Levinson on Levinson

D0764802

by the same author

SCORSESE ON SCORSESE
(with Ian Christie)

in the same series

SCHRADER ON SCHRADER
Edited by Kevin Jackson

CRONENBERG ON CRONENBERG
Edited by Chris Rodley

MALLE ON MALLE
Edited by Philip French

Levinson on Levinson

Edited by
David Thompson

faber and faber
LONDON • BOSTON

First published in 1992 in the U.K.
by Faber and Faber Limited,
3 Queen Square, London WC1N 3AU
and in the U.S. by Faber and Faber, Inc.,
50 Cross Street, Winchester, MA 01890

All rights reserved

© Barry Levinson, 1992
Introduction and editorial commentary © David Thompson, 1992

Diner © Metro-Goldwyn-Mayer Film Co. and SLM Entertainment
Barry Levinson and David Thompson are hereby identified as authors of
this work in accordance with Section 77 of the Copyright, Designs and
Patents Act 1988

CIP records for this book
are available from the British Library and the Library of Congress

ISBN 0-571-16731-4

Printed in the United States of America

31143006712187
791.4302 Lev
Levinson, Barry.
Levinson on Levinson

Contents

List of Illustrations

Acknowledgements

The interviews for this book were conducted at Barry Levinson's home in Los Angeles during one week in September 1991, when he was completing the editing of *Bugsy*. For giving generously of his time in a career that never seems to pause, much thanks are due to him, as well as for the time of his efficient office staff.

As with my endeavours on *Scorsese on Scorsese*, this book would not have been possible without the encouragement and support of its series editor, Walter Donohue. Thanks are also due to my good friends Annaliese Varaldiev and Florence Dauman, who helped a non-driver survive his first visit to Los Angeles. Important contributions were made in the field of research by Paul Kerr, Betty Leese and the staff of the irreplaceable library of the British Film Institute.

Stills and photographs appear courtesy of Barry Levinson, Rudy De Luca and the British Film Institute, as well as 20th Century Fox, Columbia Tri-Star, Warner Bros., MGM, Paramount Pictures, Touchstone Pictures and United Artists.

Barry Levinson on location for *The Natural* (1984)

Introduction

There is a scene in *Diner* – to take but one – in which Shrevie, the married man among the diner guys, bemoans the fact that he no longer has anything to discuss with his wife, Beth, since the need to worry over the problems of sex or the wedding arrangements has gone away. He says to Eddie, the next in line for marital status, 'We can sit up here and bullshit the night away, but I can't have a five-minute conversation with Beth. But I'm not putting the blame on her. We've just got nothing to talk about.'

If there are any consistent themes in Barry Levinson's work – and ones that he himself will acknowledge – they have to be the problem of communication, and the desire to avoid confrontation. In his writing-directing début, *Diner*, the spark that set him to work on the script was the realization of how little the guys he once shared his late adolescence with actually understood the opposite sex. It was an underlying element in his next Baltimore film, *Tin Men*, in which sharp-talking con-man 'B.B.' seduces his rival's wife with the ease of clinching a deal, only to find his innermost feelings directing him towards genuine affection for the unhappy woman. Even in a supposedly more mature milieu, men banter away comfortably, talking about nothing in particular, but the realities of deeper human experience may render them speechless. And that, together with endless digressions on the verity of TV shows, has become the Levinson touch.

While Barry Levinson has had one of the most successful careers around in contemporary Hollywood – two of the top-grossing films of all time and he's still up there – his very shrewdness and confidence have also managed to give just about all his work a consistent personal edge. If the obvious critical position is to take a corner with his self-penned, semi-autobiographical 'Baltimore trilogy' against the more commercial work, that would be to underestimate just how far he has touched projects initiated by other hands. *Good Morning, Vietnam* speaks of the gulf between two cultures, and the collision of humane anarchy with uptight authoritarianism; *Rain Man* tells of one young man's self-centredness shaken by feeling for someone who is denied any potential for affection and interaction. In other ways, the celebration of America as a new home in *Avalon* also permeates the golden vision of the baseball game in *The Natural*; and the pleasure of the storyteller, elaborating on a recent past that is creating its own mythology, finds a fantastic outlet in the adventures of *Young Sherlock Holmes*. *Bugsy*, too, invades the familiar territory of America's favourite myth, the gangster, and reveals a society of men whose tough, insolent modes of communication make them stand apart from the fragile domesticity that Ben Siegel allows to crumble around him.

Yet Levinson's own conscious attitude belies such neat linkage. He is something of a throwback to the classy studio director, except that the old structure no longer exists, and he has never been obliged to do hack-work. Instead, his self-effacing professionalism and often infallible nose for what will simply *work* have given him unusual respect and the power of personal choice. To hold such a position of strength, one might expect a dogmatic manipulator from the old school of directors. But instead there is an affable, private man whose real enthusiasms and complete dedication to the job in hand inspire technical departments to give of their best and his cast to reveal a genuine sense of pleasure on the screen. On set, actors have lauded his laid-backness and his appreciation of what they do. If occasionally he has tripped up on his own leanings towards warmth – those over-lyrical moments in *The Natural* or the *Casablanca*-style reconciliation in *Bugsy* – then these appear more forgivable than the blatant sentimentality of so much that Hollywood produces.

Levinson's training came in stand-up comedy and sketches, which led to years spent in the writing pool on television shows. This experience appears to have given him a fine feeling for just what is and what isn't funny. Fortunately, the one-note goofing of Mel Brooks was left behind for a closer observation of the innate humour of everyday conversations and an uncanny ability to re-create authentic speech patterns in all their excitable clumsiness and revelatory slipperiness. It would appear that Levinson has an uncommon gift for hearing voices in his head and simply letting scripts flow out, without forward planning and – even more enviable – without much tidying up. Even in his first script, . . . *And Justice for All*, written with Valerie Curtin, there is a telling scene in which Al Pacino and Christine Lahti discuss the Ethics Committee while actually seducing each other. It's the art of investing the commonplace with significance, while always avoiding pretension.

Even . . . *And Justice for All*, as Levinson himself has observed, belongs to that hallowed gallery of Baltimore films, which stand as Levinson's major achievement to date. *Diner*, for all the efforts of MGM to bury it when they realized they didn't have a bouncy little tale of high-school jinks on their hands, came upon the movie scene as a real gem. Furthermore, it was made by a director whose age saved him from 'movie brat' classification. And for all Levinson's respect and love for the classic Hollywood films, he is no hungry devourer of golden moments from the past, nor is he at all interested in playing the *hommage* game. *Diner* was a film really quite unlike any other, for it refused the nostalgia trip of *The Last Picture Show* or *American Graffiti*. Instead the film looked squarely, yet wryly, at a moment in time – the end of the 1950s and the Eisenhower era – when the characters themselves were being nostalgic. Its cast of (then) unknowns are beautifully relaxed and constantly reveal themselves in unexpected ways; Mickey Rourke is so charming and seductive, it seems to have been downhill ever since.

If *Diner* is a throwback to a time before psycho-babble changed the drift of conversations, then that accords with Levinson's own attitude to himself and his characters. His strengths lie in the small touches of life rather than the larger anxieties. Yet at the same time he combined in *Avalon* an extraordinary tapestry of family life through the century, with the encroaching commercialization of an America whose homes were infiltrated by television. Levinson likes to laugh at *TV Guide*'s summary of *Avalon*, which accuses the film of 'attacking television unfairly'. The culture of family rituals, both healthy *and* exasperating, is played off against the duping of a nation by a small flickering screen, whose stories do indeed seem paltry stuff compared to the grandfather's embellished memories. Levinson's rich blend of crack ensemble acting and finely textured period re-creation testifies to cinema's deep magic over television's tawdry banality. But there is no sense of a 'message' being delivered here, no false melodramatics; the comedy of life is always to the fore.

Even if *Diner, Tin Men* and *Avalon* were not consciously thought out as a trilogy – the director certainly hopes there are more Baltimore stories to come – there is a satisfying interweaving between them. At the close of *Diner*, Boogie agrees to pay off his debt to Bagel by joining him in the 'home improvement' business; Tilley in *Tin Men* comes to live in the house vacated by the Krichinskys; Shrevie in *Diner* buys the same Hudson once owned by the Krichinskys; and when young Michael in *Avalon* looks behind him from the family car, he sees a diner being lifted on to its site. These moments may be savoured or missed completely, but they are an indication of how important it is for Levinson that these small lives have a larger significance.

Unlike so many leading figures in Hollywood, Levinson doesn't appear to be driven by burning ambition. His attitude would seem to stem from the security of his middle-class, Jewish suburban family background, which has apparently nurtured in him the confidence simply to go forward and improve on his craft. His vocabulary is one of the artisan rather than the self-proclaimed artist – he uses words like 'work' and 'piece' a great deal – and his skill is in a finely judged control of the stylistic materials film-making offers him. *Avalon* and *Bugsy* both display a wide vocabulary of visual sleight-of-hand, but rarely is this allowed to spill over into self-admiration or unnecessary fireworks. *Toys* is clearly going to be an interesting test for him, as a fairly radical departure into comic fantasy. But then, as he recently said in a BBC Radio interview with critic Nigel Andrews, 'What I'm trying to do is better work as I go along, and challenge myself in some ways. If I see a movie so clearly that it's there, then I don't know what the challenge is, and if I don't know that, then I can't be motivated by it.'

It shouldn't be too surprising, then, that he has no interest in looking again at the films he has made, nor that for him the most enjoyable part of the process is the actual shooting – for once, a director who is not afraid of his collaborators, but positively embraces them. Of course, anyone prepared to direct Robert Redford, Dustin Hoffman and Warren Beatty is clearly no push-over. And he's certainly conjured some of the best performances around from Richard Dreyfuss, Danny DeVito, Mickey Rourke and Robin Williams. Some critics have suggested that he is weaker in dealing with women, but it's worth considering the strength revealed by Ellen Barkin in *Diner*, Barbara Hershey in *Tin Men*, Elizabeth Perkins in *Avalon*, and, of course, Annette Bening in *Bugsy*. If men are more Levinson's territory, there are signs that he understands women pretty well too. For the moment it seems that Levinson is more at home with the simple strengths of Nora than the dangerous passion of Virginia Hill, but he's clearly not wanting to close the book on the subject.

Flashback to *Diner* again: Modell in a car pondering awhile. 'You know what word I'm not comfortable with? *Nuance*. It's not really a word like gesture. *Gesture* is a good word. At least you know where you stand with *gesture* . . . But *nuance*, I don't know . . . Maybe I'm wrong.' Barry Levinson has shown that he's pretty comfortable with both.

CHAPTER I

From Baltimore to Los Angeles

Barry Levinson was born in Baltimore, Maryland, on 6 April 1942. His home was in the Jewish neighbourhood of Forest Park, where his relations had settled after emigrating from eastern Europe – mainly Poland and Russia – at the beginning of the century. The stories of that emigration and the subsequent integration into American society of the Levinsons and other families were to be celebrated forty-eight years later in his most autobiographical film, Avalon, *which would be the third movie in a loose trilogy that reflected his life in Baltimore.*

Appleton Street in south-west Baltimore was where the director's parents, Irv Levinson and Vi Krichinsky, grew up, first met and married. Memories of the district were to filter into Avalon – for example, the sign advertising his maternal grandfather Sam's profession as a paperhanger, and the circus parade that once went down the street. Irv Levinson opened the first appliance store in Baltimore, and its success meant that the young Barry grew up in a comfortable home in the suburbs, with his parents and his mother's parents, the Krichinskys.

Where I grew up was in the idyllic suburbia of the time – all trees and green lawns – from which we had to venture out to discover the major city and encounter the fights that came with territorial aspects and so on. But I lived with my parents and grandparents in the same house, so I think I saw a much wider spectrum of the adult world than most American kids of my generation. We had a lot of relatives coming through the house, some of them speaking very broken English, and I heard a lot of Yiddish. At the time it seemed quite normal to me for everybody to have a family in which some people had a hard time speaking English, and others could speak it well. And I thought everyone was hearing stories of the old country, because I had this impression that everybody had arrived from Europe at the same time – though there were others, like Lincoln, who somehow had been here for a long time! Everybody I knew had grandparents and parents with a mixture of languages.

It was my grandparents who had made the journey, and my father struggled as a young man, beginning as a salesman and then running an appliance store and a discount store. He had become very successful, so we lived in a nice neighbourhood in a comfortable home. Obviously I was a product of the evolution of the American Dream. But my generation – the second generation – had to figure out what the hell to do. I remember seeing *Rebel Without a Cause*, and identifying with that feeling of, God, what am I going to do with my life? The generation before never even had a conversation like that, because they just had to go to work to make a living to survive. Second-generation Americans suddenly thought they had it all, because everything seemed possible.

So I wandered around, not with that James Dean angst, but fairly apathetic to things taking place at school and just looking for a good time. I had very little interest in sport. I was ill during many of my early years so, in fact, I missed a lot of school. I could miss the Fifth Grade and I was still able to go to the Sixth, and then miss most of the Sixth and go on to Junior High School, and all without having to pass exams. As I figured I didn't even have to show up to pass, I really didn't feel the compulsion to work hard.

Forest Park was probably the last of those idyllic, suburban high schools with ivy-covered walls where everything seemed very simple and people did reasonably well. Very middle class, very much what the best of America could be. As I remember it, a good portion of the students went off to college, had a good education. It was when the public-school system in this country still worked. Even those who had more money wouldn't have thought of going to a private school, because you couldn't really have had a better education. But that was in the late 1950s.

1 James Dean as America's second generation in
Rebel Without a Cause (1955)

2 Barry Levinson is crowned king at the junior prom

At school, Levinson proved to be an idle student, and has claimed to have come bottom in a graduating class of 460. At the same time, however, he was apparently voted best-looking boy in the class of 1960, with the best personality, and even second-best male athlete.

I don't recall any family pressure for me to be academically successful. When I graduated from Forest Park High School, I hadn't even told my parents that I hadn't applied to college. Of course, everyone assumed you would go to college, and if you hadn't done particularly well, then you would at least go to the University of Maryland, because you had come out of a high school from that state. But I never even applied. I didn't have a great deal of ambition, nor a clue as to what I really wanted to do. I didn't even have a plan, because it never occurred to me that I would actually have to work for a living. I really was that cocooned, and life was very pleasant. Although I despised the idea of actually going to work for my father, who owned an appliance store and a carpet store at the time, at the back of my mind was the idea that I might end up doing just that. I had already worked for him on a part-time basis during the summer vacations, but I really hated the idea of selling or anything connected with it.

I had some experience after college of selling cars and encyclopedias, and of course these things turn up in my work, but I think that's because I really hated it. Even now I don't like having to go out and sell a movie, going out on a press junket. I don't think it's a moral problem, just the fact of making people want something. I wish somebody would want something because they want it, not because I convinced them. I really have no desire to convince anyone. If you want something, fine, but don't let me talk you into it.

Levinson's directorial début, Diner, *was based on memories of his regular meetings with recently graduated male friends in Brice's Hilltop Diner, located on Reisterstown Road in northwest Baltimore (and now rebuilt as a restaurant and bar). There they would drink coffee, consume French fries and gravy, smoke*

3 'Sergeants at Arms'—clockwise, David Robin, Henry Holtzman,
Matt Pollack, Bill McAuliffe and Barry Levinson (1960)
4 The 'diner guys' as portrayed in *Diner* (1982)

cigarettes and, above all, talk at great length – mainly about the local teams, the Colts and the Orioles, favourite rock 'n' roll records, gambling and, of course, girls. One of Levinson's class-mates and a diner regular was Chip Silverman, who had a cameo role in Diner, *selling clothes from the trunk of a car, and wrote a book called* Diner Guys.

I've been making a documentary over the last few years about the guys I used to meet up with in the diner, the so-called 'diner guys'. In a sense, none of them actually did hang out at the diner on a regular basis, but that's the way it seems to them now. They began to have reunions about eighteen years ago when a lot of the men would see each other again, like a sports camp weekend, and last year I filmed this joint fiftieth birthday celebration when they gathered for a roast. I'm not sure yet how this documentary will turn out, but I know it's a kind of record of the first rock and roll generation, guys who, of course, are now turning fifty.

I think at that time there was a wider spectrum of music available than there is now. When rock and roll really exploded in the 1950s, it still had really strong jazz roots. Then there were standards – guys like Sinatra, Mathis, Nat King Cole. Folk was then really beginning to be accepted. So if you had a record collection it would be made up of a lot of this kind of music. My own collection was like that, all over the place. I really liked the sound of Nat King Cole's voice, particularly when he was with a small combo, before the big orchestrations came in. And I liked a range of jazz – Charlie Parker, for example, and Louis Armstrong. I carry these sounds in my brain and, when I work, unconsciously I pluck them out. If you sit there and try to be analytical about it, I don't think you reach the same conclusions. So I leave myself always open to a certain amount of discovery.

I had decided on most of the music I wanted for *Diner*, but I brought in Allan Mason at a later stage and he's become the music supervisor on all my movies. I'll talk to him about the movie and my thoughts, and he'll suggest 600 or 700 songs, and then I'll go through them all. I'll play them, run some against the picture, and then whittle it down to maybe the eight songs that we

5 Barry Levinson and record collector Allan Mason

finally use. Mason's house is nothing but rows and rows of albums, thousands of them all around, in pristine copies. He's a really obsessive collector. He's from Baltimore, of course, and Shrevie in *Diner* is made up of Mason, Alan Barts and a couple of other people. I was never a collector on that scale, but my father sold records in his appliance store, so I had this music around me all the time.

I really wasn't any different from other kids in my neighbourhood. Every Saturday I would go to the movies in a group, just as in *Avalon*, to see the latest serial. And, of course, I would follow the usual dating pattern, taking a girl to a movie. I was also fascinated by television when it came into the house. When I began high school, and we were just getting cars, then we could go out of the neighbourhood to the Playhouse and the Five West and see European films. I loved the Ealing Comedies,[1] such as *The Ladykillers*, *The Lavender Hill Mob* and *The Man in the White Suit*. The first French film I ever saw with subtitles was *And God Created Woman*, which I don't remember too well, except that Brigitte Bardot was at that point the greatest woman I had ever seen. Her hair was all over the place, and I'd never seen a movie star look so natural – Marilyn Monroe always had so much make-up on. All this was totally different from anything else I'd seen, though of course I'm not talking as a student of films, just as a movie-goer.

I was really intrigued by the subtlety and quietness of British comedies compared with American ones, which were a lot more bang-bang and noisy. But I didn't really see the cinema as an alternative way of working. The idea of ever actually doing something myself in film or television was totally out of the question – none of us knew anybody who did that kind of thing, and something like a film school didn't exist then. I ended up graduating from high school, starting Baltimore Junior College, dropping out after five months, selling cars, going back, then selling encyclopedias, then doing a few other half-assed jobs, and deciding I was really nuts. Then I saw *The Young Philadelphians*,[2] with Paul Newman, and it really stayed in my mind. Paul Newman walking around as a lawyer – that looked interesting to me. He seemed to have fun, he was attractive to women and every-

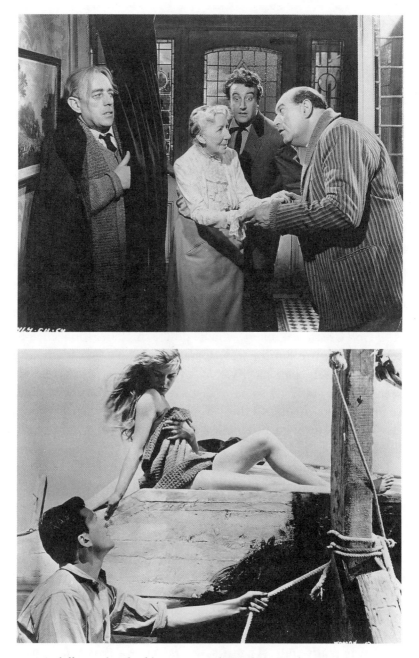

6 A different kind of humour in the Ealing Studios production,
The Ladykillers (1955)
7 Brigitte Bardot as untamed woman in Roger Vadim's
. . . And God Created Woman (1956)

8 Paul Newman's dashing young lawyer in *The Young Philadelphians* (1959)

thing else. So I decided to become an income tax lawyer. I don't know where I got the income tax part from, I'm not sure if it was in *The Young Philadelphians* or not.

I ended up coming back to this place called Mount Vernon, a college that specialized in law and where you could get a degree faster than if you spent four years in other law schools. But I found out very quickly that to be an income tax lawyer you have to understand accounting, debits and credits, and that you had to write very small with a pencil in teeny, weeny squares. Very, very difficult. I hated it and would skip classes. I didn't think about the future, that I couldn't become an income tax lawyer if I didn't attend accounting class. After I spent a few times just waiting an hour for the class to end I became bored. Around the corner from Mount Vernon was the main library for the City of Baltimore, so I drifted in there and came across the section that dealt with radio and television. I thought, oh, I like television, and picked up a book on the subject. I read books on radio, the few that were on television and the even fewer on film. Nothing about John Ford, just basic history about the origins of cinema and so on. As the year went on I read everything in the library on these subjects, and a few biographies.

Towards the end of the semester that year, we had an aptitude test. I didn't know what the hell it was for. I was told I had a high aptitude for business and a very good aptitude for the arts, which I'll never forget the teacher describing as 'that nebulous field'. He suggested, therefore, that I went into business, so I said, 'Well, no, I'm going to go into the arts.' It was a kind of youthful arrogance to say that, because I didn't even know what 'the arts' was. So I dropped out of Mount Vernon Law School, and since my grades were very poor to begin with, all I could do was return to Junior College, where they had a course on radio and television. For the first time I actually began to pay attention to things. I wanted to be a radio disc jockey. I became fascinated by the camera. I did well enough in my grades, to the point where I could complete my course at Junior College and then transfer to American University, which was supposed to be very good in Broadcast Journalism and even had a Television Department. Out of this came a job at the local television station, and that was probably one of the most exciting times I've ever had. It was like putting me in a room with every piece of equipment I could possibly play with. I now realize that much of what I do in movies was learned when I was fiddling around and experimenting back in the 1960s.

It was in 1963, while at American University in Washington, D.C., that Levinson secured his trainee job at WTOP-TV. He would do the morning news, including weather and traffic reports – which, observing that they were almost always the same, he often made up – then take a class, and return to the studio for a children's show. He served as a floor director and even worked hand puppets such as Dr Fox, Oswald Rabbit and Marvin Monkey in The Ranger Hal Show. *But most of his time was spent in the presentation area.*

No one really knew much about what to do on a local station, because you were basically providing a network feed. There was local news and promotions for programmes such as sports – this Thursday at Griffiths Stadium you can see Senator baseball, that sort of stuff. I could experiment, so I took film clips of the Washington Senators and made a tape of Dave Brubeck doing the 'Unsquare Dance'. I did all the run-downs, cutting between first and second and second and third bases, and made it like a square dance. So I was cutting the film to music, and nobody there had seen that done before. I began to play with sound, so that if you were sitting at home watching and the sound changed radically from what was before, your ear would really pay attention. It was a kind of training programme, only you could do almost anything. Often they would show old trailers for upcoming movies, like 'Bogart in *Across the Pacific*', but a lot of this stuff was destroyed so I would have to make them myself. I started to watch the movies, then I would pull pieces out of them, mix in some music to cover the transitions from one scene to another, and put in some graphic work. Of course, this was like selling the movie that was going to be on the local station. I hadn't learned any of these skills. It was literally like being in a little film library and playing around with the material.

Videotape was just beginning. With tape I realized you could jump back and forth, using some film and push a slide into it. Cutting on tape was not done electronically then. You had to put it under a magnifying glass and slice it, and if you did it wrong it had a little glitch. So I was educating myself in the bowels of this television station, and because it was also a radio station it had a huge record collection, which meant I could select all kinds of music to mix together. I was running between classes and the television station, where I worked sixty-five hours a week, so it took me a long time to graduate, if in fact I ever did – I'm still not sure.

Since it was supposed to be a training program, you ended up getting a night assignment, which was being present for *The Late Show* and *The Late Late Show*, rolling commercial breaks into the movies. So, say at 11.09 p.m. Glenn Ford walks through the door, you would fade to black, go from a commercial to a station break advertisement, announce *The Late Show*, and roll the film again – that was your job. In a week you would see at least ten films. So I began to see films that I had never seen before. For instance, *Citizen Kane*, Frank Capra, virtually all of John Ford, Howard Hawks. I first saw *Red River* on *The Late Show*, and I couldn't believe it, I just loved the film. Now, no one's telling you these are classics. So I'm sitting there with this technician next to me, and we're watching *Citizen Kane*, and I'm thinking, my God, this is amazing, and the man next to me is just saying, 'Sure, I remember seeing this when it came out.' Nothing about it being an all-time classic. I was getting goose-bumps, seeing all these films that were so great and special, and no one had prepared me for this experience. *The Late Show* was not a prestigious package, but for me it was mesmerizing. Even a film like *Casablanca*, I'd never heard about it before.

After four years of playing with all kinds of in-house promotional work for the station, the next step up was sales. Doing what I was doing was not considered a prestigious job – *that* was selling time. So there came a point when another apprentice turned up, and I just thought it was right to leave. I tinkered with

9 The shock of the old in Orson Welles's 'classic'
Citizen Kane (1941)

the idea of going into advertising, even starting an agency. But I didn't really know what the hell to do, so I went back to Baltimore for a couple of weeks and then came out to Los Angeles, with the idea of getting a job at another television station. But once I got there, the idea didn't appeal to me any more.

Levinson went west in 1967 and, despite his father's prediction that he would return to the family business within a month, his career took an unexpected turn.

I finally arrived in Hollywood because I came with someone else who was thinking of taking an acting class. I wasn't interested myself, but he said to me, 'Come on in', and I said, 'No, I'll wait outside, because I hate that bullshit.' I mean, in college you always had to be around the acting class, and it seemed to me so fake, such nonsense, very stilted, very theatrical, and I just couldn't believe in it. But I was persuaded to go in, and I saw this class at the Oxford Theater, which was led by a teacher called Jack Donner. They were doing some study work, he was questioning and provoking the students, and there was such an energy to it that I became fascinated. The whole way home I kept thinking about it, and the next day I went back and said to Jack Donner, 'I'd like to sign up for this class, but I really don't want to be an actor.' He said I couldn't come to his class and not act, that I'd have to go through the whole experience, so eventually I agreed, signed up, and stayed for over a year.

We did a lot of improvisational exercises, and it was in those that I began to realize how things were funny, how a given situation had a natural humour to it that can evolve. I remember an exercise where I was a husband and my wife wants to leave me, and though I'm happy that she's leaving, I didn't want to give that away. So I was saying, 'Honey, I really don't want you to leave, you know we can work this out', and she's packing and at the same time I'm helping her pack. I'm folding her sweater and saying, 'I really want you to stay', and going round collecting her socks, and I was getting these laughs. So Jack Donner called me over and said, 'Look, you see how with a minimal amount of work you can take this scene, which at face value seems dramatic, and subtley bring this comedy into it.' I was amazed by this, and I began to think back to those English comedies, and how they had a tendency to be a little more delicate in their approach – I could imagine Alec Guinness or Peter Sellers folding the sweater. I don't think anybody can *really* understand comedy, but I began to get an idea of what I could play with. And when I heard laughs as I was doing an improvisation, I think my mind worked like a little antenna beginning to receive a clearer signal on the radio. So I started to zero in more on the comedy side.

Craig Nelson[3] was an actor and coach at the acting school, and we used to do a lot of improvisational stuff together. After about a year, I began to rebel against some of the teaching, and wanted to try different approaches. So I ended up dropping out with Craig, and the two of us put together a comedy act, and played a few of the little clubs that were around back in the late 1960s. One of these was the Comedy Store. It was an exciting period because it was a place – and this doesn't happen a lot nowadays – where you could gather a lot of people and, while exploring your craft, interact with a group. What you walk away with may not be clearly defined, but it is there, and it will benefit your work.

With the confidence gained through this experience, Levinson and Nelson decided that they should write down many of these stage improvisations and sell them as sketches. They began working on The Lohman and Barkley Show, *which aired weekly on the local television station, KNBC-TV.*

The double act that Craig and I did led us to a writing job on the local television station, and within a few weeks we were actually performing ourselves. The producers liked a sketch about a guy on a bench, which was then part of our act, but when the actor was in rehearsal we said he wasn't going to get the laughs we did. So, this actor was a little pissed off at these writers, their first week on the show and telling him how to perform the material. He ended up doing it the way he wanted, and, sure enough, it killed a big laugh. The next week we presented a new sketch, again told the actor how we felt it should be done, and he became pissed off again. A big argument followed, but Craig and I ended up performing it, and it worked. Then we became regular performers.

The show was recorded live on tape at 9.30 p.m. and played back at 11.30 p.m. With all the flaws and disastrous routines that we did, when we watched them back at 11.30 p.m. we'd say, 'Oh God, is *that* a bad sketch.' But we were working under great pressure, with four writers producing ninety minutes of material. You'd come in on Monday morning and by Friday you had to have it finished, because Saturday would be a day off and Sunday you would rehearse and then shoot. Only you didn't really rehearse, you just kind of walked through it for the cameras. There were no refinements, so we did some terrible work, but some fascinating things came out of this situation. There was a sketch called 'The Doctors and the Vikings', and it became like a running soap opera from week to week. Quite simply, we would do a lot of doctor talk, all very dramatic and serious, and then periodically a Viking would come through the operating room, blowing his horn, look at the situation, shake his head and then leave. That was the gag, and it became very popular. Popular, that is, for a local station, with maybe the fifty people who watched it.

Then one week we decided to do an encore, called 'The Lawyers and the Pigs', with lawyers in suits speaking a lot of legalese as normal, but carrying little piglets under their arms. We'd make no reference to the piglets, and that would be the joke. When we rehearsed on the Sunday, we didn't bother to get the piglets, as we thought that was just the gag, no need to bother. When we went into the show, and it's live, we ran to find our piglets. Only these were not little piglets but huge, 70-lb pigs! I could just about carry mine to the defence table – he was so heavy – but Craig's started to crawl over his back. The judge had more sense, he actually got a piece of rope for his pig, but they started squealing and then peeing all over the stage. The audience began to laugh so loud that nobody could hear us and we couldn't hear each other. This was meant to be a quickie sketch, run two minutes and then boom and out, but it went on for thirteen minutes, with the pigs breaking free and us trying to grab hold of them, but never talking about the problem. It was absolute anarchy, with the audience screaming with laughter. People tuning in to the show were going, 'My God, they've totally gone off the deep end with this piece. This is the sickest thing on television!'

We did a sketch about a suicide prevention service, where they were always putting everybody on hold. Somebody yells, 'Hold, please. Line one, man on a ledge, line three, woman with head in oven', and we're just cutting back and forth between these phone calls. Also a quiz show called 'Beat the Chimp', where the question would be, 'What is Einstein's Theory of Relativity?' and the chimp would hit the bell first and always write out the correct answer. We were really taking chances. We would do things like signing off four minutes early as a joke. Basically, we'd say goodbye, the credits would roll, and then suddenly no more credits and we're just staring at the camera. That gag worked – sometimes they didn't. And this was 1969, some five years before *Saturday Night Live*. At that time, there was nothing really that crazy, and even *Rowan and Martin's Laugh-in* was still working in a more conventional format than we were.

Joined on this show by Rudy De Luca, Nelson and Levinson caught the attention of one Michael Ovitz with their zany performances. Now head of the powerful agency CAA, to which Levinson belongs, Ovitz hired the aspiring comedians to work on a network programme.

The next year we moved on to *The Tim Conway Comedy Hour*, which ran thirteen weeks and bit the dust. We worked as writer-performers, and did some of our crazy sketches again, such as the marching drill and precision team. Three of us would be the whole army drill team, and with great precision I'd give you the rifle, you'd give me the rifle, I'd give you the rifle, big fanfare and excitement. Another I remember was the Kamikaze pilots. How in the hell did the Japanese ever come up with the idea of Kamikaze? That was the question, and the explanation would be in Japanese gibberish, with ridiculous gestures. Pilots would be

10 Rudy De Luca, Craig Nelson and Barry Levinson
perform a sketch

lured into it by flashy clothes, shapely women or just orders from the Emperor. So we were still experimenting and playing around, trying to find things we enjoyed, always sort of left of centre. We weren't working on jokes, because our stuff didn't function as line, line, joke.

Some of this material was sent over to London, and I ended up with Rudy writing for *The Marty Feldman Comedy Machine*. It was fascinating for me, given my early love of English comedy, to be there and have someone like Spike Milligan come in from *The Goon Show*, which I had never heard of. That kind of outrageous comedy simply didn't exist in America, and we were really just scratching the surface of absurdist work ourselves. I spent about a year in England, and it was great fun working with Marty. His show ended up being butchered to death because it was too crazy for American audiences! Ironically enough, Terry Gilliam was doing animation for it, and in America they often took his contributions out because they didn't want cartoons in prime time. There were also singers and songwriters like Randy Newman[4] just sitting around playing the piano in the rehearsal hall. But they pulled out all that stuff too, in order to put in the more upbeat, zippy groups of the time, because they were supposedly more television-oriented.

On his return to Los Angeles, Levinson continued to perform sketches at the Comedy Store, where he met comedienne-writer-actress Valerie Curtin,[5] later to become his first wife. After writing for the short-lived John Byner Hour *and* Comedy News *in 1972, he had his first major break when he joined the team on* The Carol Burnett Show, *a highly popular prime-time television show that had been running since 1967. As one of the regular writers, he received two Emmy Awards, in 1974 and 1975, for the Best Writing in Variety or Music. The shows singled out were broadcast on 16 February 1974, with guests Tim Conway and Bernadette Peters, and 21 December 1974, with guest Alan Alda.*

The Carol Burnett Show was much more mainstream and therefore considered respectable. But Carol Burnett was a great sketch comedienne, and Harvey Korman did some terrific stuff

11 *The Tim Conway Comedy Hour* (1970)—Conway, Nelson,
Levinson and De Luca as Kamikaze pilots

12 *The Marty Feldman Comedy Machine* (1972) — De Luca and
Levinson (inside television set) with Feldman
13 Carol Burnett supported by Harvey Korman in her
popular TV show

with her. As sketch comedy, I think it still holds up, because they really played the material. A lot of shows at the time were done with the stars reading cue cards, like Sonny and Cher. They didn't really know how to play the comedy. People thought Sonny and Cher were pretty funny, but they were just reading off cards – neither of them really knew how to work a sketch. Carol and Harvey would work the material within the for- mat – Hi, good evening, glad you're here, sketch, sketch, guest sings a song, big sketch, goodnight. The show won two Emmys, and I was considered to be hot. Which was incredible, because I remember coming back from England and trying to get a job and whenever I mentioned Marty Feldman, no one could care less – it was a case of, oh, so tell me about the other flops you've done. So now I had done my first acceptable work.

To me, every experience you can accumulate has got to be beneficial. Some people have a natural ability and right away they can write a screenplay. I never set out to do that. From do- ing improvisations, I began to write them down, and that led to them becoming sketches, and the sketches just became a little longer. Writers of the past had lives. Most of the writers today have lives drawn from what they see on television, and that's the experience they write from, so it's like recycled work, second generation. Not real, lived experiences, but basically television experiences. And that to me isn't interesting.

Notes

1 The Ealing Comedies were a number of well-produced, memorably cast and wittily scripted films made in London in the late 1940s and early 1950s under the supervision of Ealing Studios head Sir Michael Balcon. Among the most successful were *Whisky Galore* (1949), *The Man in the White Suit* (1951) and *The Ladykillers* (1955), all of which were directed by Alexander Mackendrick (b. 1912), who later left for Hollywood and made the cult film *Sweet Smell of Success* (1957). Levinson is a keen fan of Mackendrick's work – he even professes a liking for the director's unhappy last film, *Don't Make Waves* (1967). Two of Levinson's films contain tributes to *Sweet Smell of Success*: a character in *Diner* has learned the entire script

(which was by Ernest Lehman and Clifford Odets) by heart, and the film is watched on television by Raymond in *Rain Man*.

2 *The Young Philadelphians* (1959), directed by Vincent Sherman, starred Paul Newman as a poor lawyer with ambitions who defends an army friend on a murder charge and woos a society girl.

3 Better known as Craig T. Nelson, he later found a movie career as a straight actor, notably in *Poltergeist* (1982) and *Silkwood* (1983).

4 Randy Newman, nephew of Hollywood composer Alfred Newman, has established himself as a witty and ironic popular songwriter/singer, and has also worked successfully as a film composer. He wrote the song 'Gone Dead Train' for *Performance* (1970), was nominated for an Oscar for his score for *Ragtime* (1981), and co-wrote, as well as supplied the songs for, the Steve Martin–Chevy Chase–Martin Short comedy *Three Amigos* (1986). For Barry Levinson he has written the scores for *The Natural* and *Avalon*.

5 Valerie Curtin began her career in a Los Angeles improvisational group in 1972, and then appeared as a Beatnik Russian poetess in the TV series *Happy Days*. Cast by Martin Scorsese as the inept waitress in *Alice Doesn't Live Here Anymore* (1975), she subsequently acted in *Silver Streak* (1976), *Silent Movie* (1976) and *All the President's Men* (1976). She wrote scripts for *The Mary Tyler Moore Show* and *Phyllis*, and acted in the TV series *Nine to Five*.

CHAPTER 2

From Mel Brooks to *Diner*

It was Ron Clark, a producer on The Tim Conway Show, *who thought up the original idea of* Silent Movie, *and felt that Levinson and Rudy De Luca would be the ideal co-writers for it. So began a regular series of meetings with Mel Brooks, mostly held over a table with a tape recorder at a Jewish delicatessen, Factor's Famous Deli, on Pico Boulevard. The New York-born Brooks had made his name through night-club appearances, recordings and several TV series, including* Get Smart. *His notoriously tasteless Jewish humour eventually found its way into the movies with the cult success of* The Producers *(1968), followed by* The Twelve Chairs *(1970) and the Western spoof* Blazing Saddles *(1973), a huge hit that was quickly followed up by the horror spoof* Young Frankenstein *(1974).*

Mel Brooks had long been a hero of mine; his '2,000-year-old Man' album just used to kill me, destroy me. Ironically enough, it was Ron Clark, who had been a producer on *The Tim Conway Show* some four years before, who called up, saying, 'I've got a great idea for a movie – a silent movie. We're going to be with Mel Brooks on this idea, and if he's interested, maybe we could bring you guys in, because he thinks there's going to be a lot of writers.' We were pretty good with visual jokes, so we were interested. Then he called back two hours later, saying, 'Mel loves the idea and wants to do the movie. Can he meet you guys tomorrow?' We went over to see him and that was it – suddenly we were going to do this silent movie.

We were still working on *The Carol Burnett Show*, so we would meet at lunch-times in a deli, and there we would write. It took a long time, but Mel was great to be around, funny and smart. It became a very collaborative effort. You might have a

14 Slapstick revisited by Dom DeLuise, Marty Feldman and
Mel Brooks in *Silent Movie* (1976)

particular visual joke that was yours, but you didn't take any pride of ownership.

The resulting film, Silent Movie, *was released in 1974. True to its title, it was entirely silent except for music and occasional sound effects, and one brief vocal contribution from Marcel Marceau. This began a period of apprenticeship in the movie business for Levinson, with Mel Brooks as his patron. His next screen credit was to be in Brooks's pastiche of Hitchcock,* High Anxiety.

I remember we talked a lot about jokes. When we were writing *High Anxiety*, one of the things that I thought funny that never got into the film was to do a take-off of the crop-dusting scene in *North by Northwest*. Not the scene itself, but to do the scene before, because what I find so crazy about it is the planning – We've got to kill Thorndyke. What shall we do? I've got it, why don't we have him take a bus to the middle of a corn field, hire a plane, find a pilot, get somebody to operate a machine-gun, then we'll gun him down? So they've just stabbed somebody to death in the United Nations building, now they've got to get a plane, grow a whole cornfield, the whole operation – I just love that.

Levinson had previously acted a cameo role in Silent Movie *as a movie executive, but Brooks offered him a speaking part in* High Anxiety, *as an irate hotel bellboy who attacks the central character in his shower with a rolled-up newspaper.*

My acting role came out of making fun not of the shower murder itself in *Psycho*, which is obviously brilliant, but the Bernard Herrmann music. One day I was saying how his music is very close to screaming, and I basically imitated Herrmann's music, because I was fascinated by the frequency he was using and how effective it was in blurring the line between screaming and music. And Mel said, 'Well, you're the only one that has a voice that's that high, so you'll have to do it.' So that's how I ended up doing it.

15 The well planned crop-dusting scene in Alfred Hitchcock's
North by Northwest (1959)

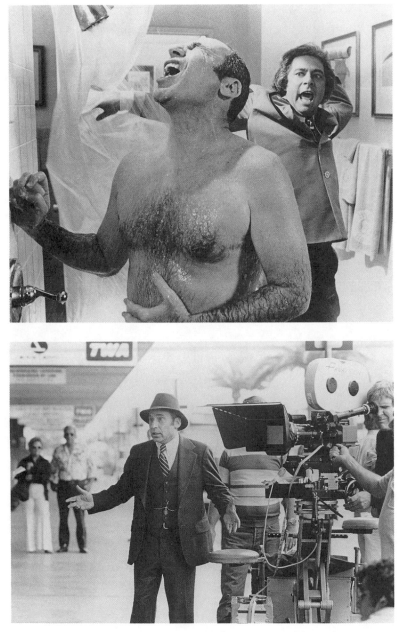

16 Levinson as the angry bell-hop in Mel Brooks's
High Anxiety (1977)
17 Mel Brooks directs himself in *High Anxiety* (1977)

While doing *Silent Movie* we were still writing for Carol Burnett, so we couldn't be on the set all the time. But on *High Anxiety* we were involved full-time, and I'd be on the set every day. It was then that I got my first experience of watching a movie being made, on a day-to-day basis. For all the technique that you have, you've also got to be prepared for the duration of a movie, the stamina of being there and handling all the things that come up and feed into the making of that movie. Because there's no real right and wrong to some of it. The camera would be over here and I would wonder, gee, should this scene play a little faster, should he throw the line away when he goes to the door rather than turning back, and so on. So suddenly the mind starts finding all these other ways and other possibilities.

Sometimes I would speak out, because Mel was very open, and you could say, 'Mel, I really think you should do this.' And he used to make a big to-do – 'Oh, now he wants to *direct*' – and he'd try to embarrass you. But he would listen. I didn't try to interfere in terms of camera positions and movement, because everybody has a different sensibility, and Brooks has his own particular style of working. But I began to think about camera placement, and music too in some cases. I never really thought seriously about directing, I was just having ideas.

Levinson's association with Mel Brooks brought him into contact with Mark Johnson, who was to become producer on all the films Levinson directed after Diner. *Born in Washington, D.C., Johnson had graduated from the University of Virginia and spent two years at the University of Iowa Film School. Eventually he moved to New York, where he was accepted into the Directors' Guild training programme and worked in various capacities on such films as* Next Stop, Greenwich Village *(1976),* Movie Movie *(1978),* The Brink's Job *(1978) and* Escape from Alcatraz *(1979).*

Mark Johnson was second assistant director on *High Anxiety*. We met then, but a couple of years went by before we actually got together as a producer–director team. I think we have a successful partnership because we're so different. It's not a competitive situation, just that he's able to deal with areas that I don't want to know about. I don't like to talk to studio people much. It's not that I wish to make an issue of it or that I'm really temperamental – I'm just not good at meetings. I don't want to have enthusiastic conversations about what I am doing and how I am going to do it. You know, 'Oh gosh, isn't this going to be wonderful!' I really prefer not to talk like that, and I find that the fewer associations I have to make, the better off I am.

With High Anxiety *completed, Levinson decided that he wanted to concentrate on his own brand of comedy, and he began writing scripts with Valerie Curtin, whom he married in December* 1977.

I believe this was the first time that I really began to think about where I was going. I realized that I'd just be known as a Brooks writer, and much as I enjoyed doing those films, I had no great love for that funny, burlesque type of movie, which was wonderful for Mel but not for me. So I wanted to get as far away as I could from them, to dispel that perception of me. So I suddenly hit on the idea of . . . *And Justice for All*, which was provoked by a car accident which had simply involved a cracked tail light, and then eight months later I had found myself being sued. I felt pretty angry about that. Valerie and I ending up writing what was a kind of dark piece. I had written down my first idea for the movie, in which the main character had a brother called Arthur, who was a lawyer, and this lawyer was divorced from his wife; he felt his life was falling apart. He was only a minor character, and I was talking to somebody about it, and he said, 'You know, you ought to get rid of him, he's not important.' And I said, 'What do you mean, he's not important in the movie? He's very important. You can make a whole movie just about this guy, a lawyer who's disillusioned with the legal system.' Then I began to think about it, and I remember talking with Valerie, and I said I thought we could write a movie about Arthur.

I decided I needed to get more inside the legal system to understand what was going on and the absurdities that existed. I knew one of the diner guys who had become a lawyer, so I went back

18 The original poster design for . . . *And Justice for All* (1979)

to Baltimore and talked to him. He told me about a lot of case histories, and then I hung around the court-houses and saw what was going on, from people lost in the system to lawyers who became confused because they didn't know which cases they had, or because they'd never even seen their clients prior to a case. So all of this craziness began to emerge, and we started to fashion the script after that. Everything in the script was based on actual cases, though we were later criticized that it was an absurdist view of the legal system. All these events actually happened, from the three days' difference between new evidence to the judge who carried a gun and fired it in court. Now I read that more and more judges are carrying guns.

I wasn't thinking about directing it myself. We just wrote the screenplay from scratch and sold it. Then a producer became involved, and he found Norman Jewison to direct, and Jewison brought in Al Pacino. In retrospect, . . . *And Justice for All* could have been one of the Baltimore stories, because it was like a diner guy who evolved into a lawyer, and it's almost a sequel to *Diner*. It's twenty years later and this guy's become frustrated with the system and his marriage is falling apart – and originally there was more about that in the script. So it would have dealt with the disillusionment of that period versus the idealism of the 1950s, and you would have seen the twenty-year gap. But I hadn't thought about the Baltimore pieces yet.

I had no real idea how to write a screenplay. With me, it's always been instinctively a matter of how you hear things. I feel how the characters talk, and I just write it down. I don't consciously try to say what a character would be able to do. All writers find a certain voice that works for them, discover a rhythm to it all. I've always been very strong on dialogue, period. My feeling has always been that the dialogue is in fact action if you handle it correctly, and you don't need to 'employ' some kind of visual circus to keep the audience involved. If you can kick it right, then people become involved in it. Some of the older directors knew it well, and they just kept you fascinated. There was no need to say, 'Look at me, I'm the director, I know these actors are working but I'm the director.' If you handle dialogue well, give energy to it, show the shadings of it, then it's ex-

19 Al Pacino as the disillusioned lawyer in
. . . And Justice for All (1979)

citing. I never consciously thought this out. These things just get into your system – or they're in your system, I don't know which. Now I think back, when I saw *The Thing*[1] as a kid, one of the things that amazed me was all these people talking. I know it's supposed to be a creepy, scary movie, but I loved those people all talking at one another, with the dialogue overlapping.

Levinson and Curtin were nominated for an Academy Award for Best Original Screenplay for . . . And Justice for All *and consequently became an established Hollywood writing team. Their next collaboration was to be an adaptation of Todd Walton's novel about a crippled Vietnam veteran discovering a new life amongst a family of social misfits who meet up in a bar,* Inside Moves.

I believe the studio had this novel, and we read it and found it interesting. Then Richard Donner read it and he became involved. When we wrote *Inside Moves*, I still had no thoughts about directing. But when I walked on the set, I knew that it was going to be a different movie from the one I had in my head. That's the dilemma of the writer, because it's not as they say, that the words are everything; the room and the colour and how you light it ultimately have to be connected to the dialogue in some fashion. When I saw that room I realized the difference, because the characters were close to the bar, just a few feet away, and if they were that close they were not really outcasts. I had pictured a long bar and way down the far end, in this darkened room, would be a table of misfits. They were not a close family in that respect – you would have to walk to them and back from them. I realized that *Inside Moves* was going to be a warmer movie than I had thought it would be.

I remember when I started to write *Diner*, I wished I hadn't already used one piece of dialogue in *Inside Moves*, where they were talking about Dillinger, and how his penis was being exhibited in a jar. It was perfect diner talk, because it was like a conversation we had: 'What, you mean it was actually in a jar?' 'Well, somebody said it was, they hadn't seen it.' 'Well, it's probably on tour. You know they toured those things', and so on. It

20 Drama through dialogue in the Howard Hawks production
The Thing (From Another World) (1951)
21 The community of misfits and cripples in *Inside Moves* (1980)

was diner talk, but here it wasn't tossed off in the same fashion. Then I began to think about directing, because I realized that there was a real difference of approach here, and maybe I could try to do that.

Levinson's directorial début was to be another original screenplay by himself and Curtin, Toys. *It was set up at 20th Century Fox with Mark Johnson as producer, but at the last minute a new studio regime cancelled the film. In 1981 Valerie Curtin was away on an acting assignment for a month and, with time to spare, Levinson spent three weeks writing the script of* Diner, *a distillation of the days spent with his friends at the Hilltop Diner. The encouragement to write this particular script came out of those regular meetings with Mel Brooks.*

I had a lot of stories in my mind about my Baltimore friends, mostly incidents and anecdotes. Mel Brooks used to tell me that I ought to write them into a movie. He said they reminded him of the Fellini film, *I Vitelloni*,[2] which I hadn't seen. But while I thought these things were funny, I often didn't know what they were about, and the idea of putting together some comedy piece didn't appeal. Then one day it occurred to me that all these stories were about *women*. When I figured that out, I realized why we guys behaved the way we did; that the whole idea of hanging out at the diner together created this amazing naïveté in terms of women, and then I could begin to try and deal with it.

In terms of our group, you would never bring your date into the diner. You could go across the street to Mandel's Deli and take your date there, but you dropped her off before coming over to the diner. That was our crazy sensibility. There were times when you would be out with your date and you wouldn't be that crazy about her, so you would drive by the diner to see which guys were there from their cars parked outside. If you thought, wow, something good's going on, then you'd drop her off and come back to the diner. When all this made sense, I could sit right down and start to write it. And I wrote it very quickly.

I think the dialogue in *Diner* is constantly about women and the guys' inability to understand them, their neglect of them. It's

22 Aimless young men at play in Federico Fellini's *I Vitelloni* (1953)
23 'Boogie' (Mickey Rourke) and his date in *Diner* (1982)

funny, but once that went into my brain, all of a sudden it brought up other things, such as Shrevie's record collection. His incomprehension at his wife not understanding how important it is to keep them in order and know them backwards, and vice versa – all these things kept interconnecting in one way or another. That's what we strived for in the film, because there isn't a top-heavy kind of story making where you hang on to what's supposed to happen every moment; it was a behavioural kind of piece.

I used a number of favourite slang expressions to add a certain colour to the dialogue – such as a great-looking person was 'death'. When Fenwick says he's going to Europe because it 'looks like a smile', he means it's something that could be interesting. When you're writing, you're never sure what will go over or connect, but here it makes sense that he reduces it, rather than saying, 'If I go to Europe, it could be really interesting.' Saying it could be a 'smile' to the girl, it's as much as he is willing to give of his feelings to someone. I don't know if she even understands the way he talks, but this language cuts through with a certain ring that I like.

Many of the characters in Diner *are close to Levinson's actual contemporaries. Boogie was based on a real Boogie, who was famed for handling himself well in fights. There was a legendary Earl, who could consume in one sitting everything listed on the left-hand side of the menu. And Eddie was based on Levinson's cousin, Eddie Kirk, who liked to sleep late into the afternoon and, when he got out of bed, would pull on last night's shirt which he hadn't bothered to unbutton.*

As to the structure of the impending wedding, I made a lot of that up, as my cousin Eddie didn't get married at that time, although he did give his bride-to-be a football test. Looking for something to make all these incidents hang together, I decided they would ultimately lead up through a five-day period to the wedding. So this time period gave it an urgency, though I didn't want to type the film or jam plot devices into it. The last five days

24 The guys gather round 'Eddie' (Steve Guttenberg) at
the wedding in *Diner* (1982)

of 1959 seemed to me to hold it together, as opposed to spreading events over a year, which wouldn't have had the edge I wanted.

Initially, I didn't think of not showing Eddie's bride. It was later on that I thought, gee, she never turns up in these scenes, and because we talk about her, I realized we might as well just keep her out. In some way she was representational, so there was no sense in introducing her as a character later in the movie. Then, all of a sudden we have expectations, so the idea was to hold them off, and then, when at the wedding she throws the bouquet, the other characters would see only her back anyway! So it wasn't that I tried to find ways to avoid showing her, it simply evolved that way.

I don't know how to write with an outline structure. I have to work from the characters, not a structure into which I then try and put the characters. I get the ideas in my head, and then at a certain point I begin and just go until I get to the end. I try to work as quickly as possible in a fairly regimented way, starting around 10.30 in the morning and writing until 1.30, breaking for lunch, and then I'll write until 6.00 or 7.00 in the evening. I'll play music[3] constantly until I get there, trying to go as fast as possible, because all these voices are talking and these events happening and I'm just trying to keep up with it. In a sense I'm just taking dictation, but I have to race through because one scene starts suggesting other scenes. Sometimes I've had an idea, but I don't necessarily know how to put it in, and then all of a sudden I go, wow, that will tie right into this, and this feeds into that. That's the way I work. If I had to write an outline, then I would still be writing the outline for *Diner*!

With the collapse of Toys, *Mark Johnson had moved to become head of production for Jerry Weintraub. Excited by the script of* Diner, *he showed it to his boss. Weintraub was sufficiently enthusiastic to set the film up with MGM in a matter of days. At the age of thirty-nine, Levinson was given his first movie to direct, with a free hand in choosing his young cast.*

The casting was mostly unknowns at the time. Mickey Rourke was chosen for *Body Heat* after he was cast in *Diner*, but *Body*

Heat was released before. Daniel Stern had a couple of credits, including *Breaking Away*, but mainly they were all young actors coming up. When I did a film test of Ellen Barkin, Jerry Weintraub had a fit, saying she wasn't good-looking enough. But I saw about 500 or 600 actors in all, whittling them down to the five main guys and Ellen.

I think I approached the actors much as I've continued to do. I basically leave everything as loose as possible, not feeling that I've got to push the actors around or have them do something a given way, even though there is a way I want it to be done and a certain rhythm that I want the whole piece to have. I want to let things evolve in a very easy-going atmosphere so that the behaviour suddenly starts happening. I don't like to rehearse a lot. There are certain directors who like to have extensive rehearsal periods, then do a couple of takes and move on. For me personally, I find that nice, professional work which doesn't have an edge to it seems too pat. I prefer to let the actors be almost struggling with their lines and worrying about how they are going to cope with certain things, and then out of the takes that we are doing you shape a kind of behaviour. If you're doing *The Hunchback of Notre Dame*, then you're going to need some rehearsal because you're creating a character, but if, as in the case of *Diner*, you are selecting certain actors who are not so far removed from the characters, then they are in the ball park already. So you want them to sneak up on that behaviour without feeling they have to do lots of acting.

I learned some important things on *Diner*. I'm about to direct my first film, and I've got a production designer who's supposed to be good, so I say, he'll just take me right to these locations I've described – Eddie's house or whatever – and that will be it. And I'm looking at the place, and he's showing me the bedroom, the kitchen and so on, and I'm thinking to myself, I don't know where to shoot this scene, I don't know where to put the camera. So we go to the next location, and he says, 'This room will be fabulous', and I still don't know where to put the camera or where anybody's going to move. I'm thinking to myself, oh my God almighty, I don't know how to do anything, I don't know how to stage this, I don't know where the camera goes, I'm to-

25 'Shrevie' (Daniel Stern) and Beth (Ellen Barkin) in *Diner* (1982)

26 Levinson directs his young cast (Steve Guttenberg and Timothy Daly) in *Diner* (1982)

tally in the dark. And he's saying, 'This is a great spot!' So we come to another location and I walk in, and the second I walk in it's like I'm watching the scene. I went, 'Cameras over here, and he crosses to there, like that.' Everything makes sense, so I finally said to myself, that is the way it works, this is the way I'm going to work. When you show me a place and I know where everything goes, that's the location. So I said to him, 'Those other two locations are out. Find something else.' Then I would just keep going, and when I would see places that I understood, those are the ones I would use, and when I didn't know how to shoot it, those wouldn't do.

Interestingly enough, there are a million decisions you make as a director, right and wrong, whatever they may be. But these are the moments that stand out – especially as a young director (although I was already in my late thirties, so I wasn't *really* young). We had a diner picked out, but there were problems because we were on a highway and we had to have the traffic shut down. Still, we were going to use it, until the guy tried to charge us more money for it and the budget didn't allow for it, so it was getting to be a mess. My cinematographer was Peter Sova, and despite the fact Peter's Czech and didn't speak English so well then, we got along well. In fact, of all the cinematographers I've worked with, somehow I feel closest to him, because I think he understands me in a way no other cinematographer does. We were driving around Baltimore and we came upon this little piece of land right on the waterfront, with the city in the background. And I said, 'Boy, look at this, Peter. What a place for the diner!' It was perfect, with all the stuff right by the water's edge, and the streets on the other side looking very picturesque and very period, so I wouldn't have to spend any money trying to fix anything up.

I talked to Mark Johnson, who was producing, and said, 'We need to find our own diner and then put it on this property, instead of paying the other guy all this money he's charging us.' He said, 'Well, maybe it's possible.' The production designer tells us there's a diner graveyard in Oakland, New Jersey, so we start walking round there and I see this diner, half in the mud because it's wintertime, and it's perfect. The City of Baltimore gives us the land, so one morning we have to lay a little foundation for the diner. We're doing this with some cinder blocks, and the production designer says something about looking out of the window and seeing the lights on the water. But I point out that it can't be so, because when you look out of the window of a diner you see the streets, so how is it possible to see the water? He says, 'Well, the diner faces the water, because it's very picturesque. You look outside and see the lights of the city.' I say, 'But how do I see the diner, then? I'd have to be in a canoe somewhere! I mean, trucks go by diners, cars go by diners, you see the diner with its sign. What's the point of a diner in the middle of the harbour? At night-time, it will be so black you won't see anything except little dots of light. It won't mean anything.' But the designer's assistant keeps saying, 'Oh, but it will be wonderful', and everyone keeps agreeing. And I'm standing there, just beside myself. I haven't made a movie before, and I've got a diner facing the harbour!

So I finally said, 'No, the diner faces the street. You pull in because it's a diner, that's the way it faces', and I left. And I'm thinking, I don't know, this guy's done a lot of movies, but I've got to go with my instinct that I don't understand it facing the other way. So it's the first moment I really have to step up and say, 'No, look, here's the way I see this, this is the movie that I have to make. Right or wrong ultimately, at some point you have to step up, otherwise you're lost, you might not make the movie you see. And that was a moment of testing, in terms of my work and what I was focusing on. I had to go on my intuitive feeling that this is what is right. In a sense it's the only thing that I've used as a guideline. In everything I've done, I can only go with what seems to make sense to me.

Notes

1   *The Thing (From Another World)*, released by RKO in 1951, was the sci-fi/horror story of scientists at an Arctic station digging up a frozen alien. Despite some shock moments, the film is notable for its witty and fast-

paced dialogue scenes, and as a result its direction, though credited to Christian Nyby, is more often thought to be the work of the producer, Howard Hawks.

2 *I Vitelloni* (1953), Federico Fellini's first international success, dealt with the lives of five aimless young men in a small Adriatic town, and used a free, anecdotal structure to describe their coming to terms with adulthood.

3 Reportedly, one of the records Levinson played during the writing of *Diner* was Pete Townshend's 'Empty Glass'. For *Tin Men*, it was Nat King Cole's 'Sweet Lorraine' and Frank Sinatra's 'In the Wee Small Hours'.

CHAPTER 3

From *Diner* to *Young Sherlock Holmes*

Diner was made for a budget of $5.5 million, and Levinson finished on schedule and $500,000 under budget. Despite the acclaim that was to come, including an Academy Award nomination for Best Original Screenplay, the film had trouble finding its true (and highly appreciative) audience. A lot of this was down to misunderstandings about the style of the film, and its daring in being based on character and dialogue rather than plot or obvious comedy.

Sometimes we changed things in the script of *Diner* because new ideas introduced themselves into the piece, but predominantly it was written in a loose behavioural fashion. Sometimes people want to say something, but they go sideways to get to the point, and I enjoy that in terms of writing. I think that's very much how we function, especially when we have a certain amount of emotion at stake. We have a tendency often not really to hit the nail on the head, and as I like to be off-centre, there is a certain kind of coloration that creeps in. So in my writing, it's a stylistic thing.

I remember I finally showed a cut of the movie to an MGM executive, who said, 'You know, you have a lot to learn about film-making.' I said, 'I'm sure I do, but can you give me an example?' He said, 'Well, like in the roast-beef scene. He asks for the roast beef and they go on and on about the roast beef. Instead: he asks for the roast beef, then boom, you cut, finish that beat and move on to the next beat. Just move on, and get to the story. And I said to him, 'That is the story, that's basically it! What they're talking about is their relationship and their friendship. That's what it's all about and it's done by talking about roast beef.' It was a very difficult time to make someone understand this. I think the studio let me make the movie because they thought it was about high-school students, as opposed to guys who were basically out of college already.

17. Interior. Diner.

Angle on the GUYS *in the booth*

MODELL: (*To* EDDIE) What's that, roast beef?

EDDIE: Don't ask me this any more, Modell. Yes.

MODELL: Gonna finish that?

EDDIE: Yeah, I'm gonna finish it. I paid for it; I'm not going to give it to you.

MODELL: Because if you're not gonna finish it, I would eat it . . . but if you're gonna eat it –

EDDIE: What do you want? Say the words.

MODELL: No . . . if you're gonna eat it, you eat; that's all right.

EDDIE: Say the words: 'I want the roast-beef sandwich.' Say the words, and I'll give you a piece.

SHREVIE: Will you cut this out. I mean, every time!

EDDIE: He doesn't talk.

SHREVIE: But you know what he means, right?

EDDIE: Yeah, I know what he means . . . but he beats about the bush . . . He beats about the bush. If he said the words, I'd give him a piece.

MODELL: If I wanted it, wouldn't I ask?

EDDIE: Then ask. You know you want it.

SHREVIE: Will you let it go!

MODELL: You're an annoying asshole.

EDDIE: I'm annoying? I'm trying to eat a meal by myself.

SHREVIE: If you want to give him the sandwich, give him the sandwich. If you don't want to give him the sandwich, don't.

EDDIE: I don't want to . . . Look at his eyes.

MODELL: I asked one, simple question . . . You know, the trouble with you, you don't chew your food . . . That's why you get so irritable. You've got lumps . . . You've got like roast beef that just stays there.

EDDIE: Modell! Now you're really, really getting me mad. Now my blood is boiling.

SHREVIE: I'll take the sandwich. (*He leans over to* EDDIE's *plate and picks up the roast-beef sandwich.*)

EDDIE: You see . . . You do this every time.

MODELL: Why are you blaming me? He took your sandwich. I'm sitting here having a cup of coffee . . .

SHREVIE: (*To* EDDIE) You want this? You want this?

EDDIE: (*Getting madder*) No, no!

FENWICK: I do.

EDDIE: I can't believe this. You two play against me; that's what the problem is. You're on each other's sides.

There were a lot of misunderstandings. They opened it first in what they call test cities, which means sending the movie out to die in Phoenix and St. Louis. It was so misunderstood in terms of what it was supposed to be, I was shocked. I mean, it was like the most foreign film, and MGM tried to advertise it like some high-school hangout movie. 'There is a little place called the Diner where Eddie and the guys hang out' – that kind of trailer which makes you gag. So the movie soon closed in these test cities. Then Judith Crist was having a film weekend and she was supposed to show some Blake Edwards films, with *Victor/Victoria* as the latest. But this film wasn't ready, or at least they thought so, so she was stuck without a new film. Someone at MGM who liked *Diner*, but had been told not to show it around, suggested she screen this as my first movie and complement it with . . . *And Justice for All* and the Mel Brooks movies. Since he had arranged this screening for her, he invited other critics along. Judith Crist was happy to take it for her weekend. The other critics liked it too, and asked, 'When's the movie coming out, because we're really high on it?' Pauline Kael was among them; she's hated everything I've done since, but she did like that one movie. The guy from MGM said he didn't know when it would be released, and these critics said they would run their reviews anyway. As MGM didn't want to look bad, they quickly decided to open *Diner* at the Festival Theater in New York, as the movie playing there, *I'm Dancing as Fast as I Can*, wasn't doing well, and they had two weeks to get rid of.

So *Diner* finally opened in New York on a Friday in the spring of 1982, with these great reviews from *The New York Times, The New Yorker* and *Rolling Stone*. After a very good Friday, on Saturday night there was a huge rainstorm. I was staying at the Sherry-Netherland a block away, in Sydney Pollack's suite, where I was doing some rewrites on *Tootsie*, and from there I could see if there was a line on the corner. Sydney noticed that I was looking out at the rainstorm and couldn't see anybody on the corner, so he tried to make me feel good, saying, 'You know, it's very hard to get people to stand in the rain.' I had to take a cab to dinner and riding by I couldn't see anybody in front of the theatre, so my heart dropped. Then I met Mark Johnson at dinner, and he said, 'Did you stop by the theatre? And I replied, 'No, I didn't have the heart.' He said, 'Well, it's sold out.' I said, 'Sold out! I didn't see anybody.' He said they'd let the queue come in and take shelter downstairs. So it had a huge Saturday, sold out all shows on Sunday, and one of the MGM people at the theatre told me that it was very good and if it took $4,000 on a weekday, then it would have some staying power.

I flew back to Los Angeles, and then the theatre had a very good Monday. Tuesday there's a blizzard in New York and I'm thinking, oh my God, but anyway I call the theatre and say, 'Hi, this is Barry Levinson, just checking out the movie for the day.' They tell me it's $6,500! That weekend it broke the house record for the Festival, and then the movie went to another theatre and had a huge run. But the studio was still hesitant about releasing the movie wide because they said it might not travel. So they went to Boston. Extremely good first week, broke the house record in the second. Same thing in Toronto, then in San Francisco. In Los Angeles they didn't want it to go into Westwood; they said, 'Maybe an art-house in Wilshire.' They told me it would be killed in Westwood, but I battled with them, pointing out it was not an inaccessible movie and that this had been proven. In the final analysis they never did let the movie play wide in the United States. They never had more than 200 prints working here because they were so adamant that it was not going to succeed, and nothing was going to change their minds.

Then CBS approached me and said they would like to do *Diner* as a television series. I said, 'Are you going to test it?' Because if they tested it, it wasn't going to do well; so I said if they were, then why didn't they save their money. We'll say it doesn't test well and that will be the end of it. They said, 'No, no. We understand it's different. We want to try a new programme.' I went and made the pilot, on film and on location, and it was unusual for its time because it had no laugh track, and there had never been a half-hour that was sort of a drama/comedy. Anyway, they tested it after all and then said, 'Well, it doesn't test well.' It was never aired and that was the end of that. I received a letter from CBS saying how proud they were because a reviewer had said that it was too good for television! I've not had a lot of success in television, but I thought the show had potential. Of course, its form has now come to television, and it probably should have been an hour show, like a much more humorous *thirtysomething*,[1] dealing with transition and marriage and settling down and responsibilities. But at that particular time there was nothing like it and CBS said it was not compatible with their other programming. Like, I have to worry about a lot of shows apart from the one I'm doing!

While the delays in distribution affected Diner, *which went on to make about $25 million, the scripts that Levinson and Valerie Curtin had written were being put into production. Eventually emerging as a comedy vehicle for Burt Reynolds and Goldie Hawn,* Best of Friends *had as its basis the relationship between two writers not dissimilar to Levinson and Curtin. In the film, the couple decide to marry secretly and then visit their respective in-laws to tell them the news, with fairly disastrous consequences.*

Best of Friends was written before *Diner* but picked up afterwards. Again, it could have been a Baltimore story, because it was really dealing with Valerie Curtin and myself being writers. Of course, we turned it into something else, but it was semi-autobiographical. It could have been about somebody from Baltimore who's going to California to sort out his writing and his personal relationships and his family, but then it wouldn't have been quite as much of a star vehicle. I think it was Norman Jewison who settled on Buffalo in Virginia as the parental home rather than Baltimore, probably because having made . . . *And Justice for All* in Baltimore he wanted another city. I wasn't crazy about the finished film. It didn't seem like something that I was ever involved in, although it did connect with a lot of things going on in our lives at the time. The movie-producer figure with his running shoes and all his bullshit, he was very close to reality. So much so that when the guy read it, he didn't even realize it was him.

27 Goldie Hawn and Burt Reynolds as the writing couple in
Best of Friends (1982)

Unfaithfully Yours was a reworking of one of the last films to be written and directed by Preston Sturges, a bitter comedy of the same title starring Rex Harrison and Linda Darnell and released by 20th Century Fox in 1948. Although not as perfectly realized as Sturges's earlier films for Paramount, such as The Lady Eve *(1941) and* Sullivan's Travels *(1941), there is a deft performance by Harrison as a world-famous conductor – said to be modelled on Sir Thomas Beecham – who, in the course of a concert, dreams of three possible ways of murdering his supposedly unfaithful wife.*

The reason Valerie and I became fascinated with the project was that it was going to be written for Peter Sellers. Of course, I was a big fan of Sellers from the English comedies I had enjoyed as a kid, and I thought he would really handle the jealousy and also have dignity as a conductor. We wrote it, Sellers died of a heart attack, then Dudley Moore was involved, and things changed from my original ideas. I like Preston Sturges a lot, but I don't think the original *Unfaithfully Yours* is a good film at all. A good idea but not a good movie – not that the remake was a particularly good movie either. Our idea was to play with the music throughout in terms of the conductor's fantasies, rather than having just one fantasy. So he would be riding in his limo, listening to music, and suddenly he would look out of the window and he would fantasize that he sees his wife on a street corner making out with someone. So the music conjured up the images of his fantasies.

There was a scene we wrote supporting this, so that when he conducted we were already going with the fantasies – which was a different way to play it from Sturges and, I thought, a fun departure. He was composing at the piano and playing a video of the scene where his wife as an actress comes into the room and she's kissing someone. Only the way he sees it, she's French kissing him, moving her hand over him, and while he's studying this video for clues, he's changing notes in the score. Then, when he's conducting this music on the sound stage for this romantic scene, every time she touches the man it would sound like the music from *Psycho*, a kind of harsh, dissonant sound against what is

28 Linda Darnell, Kurt Kreuger and Rex Harrison in Preston
Sturges's *Unfaithfully Yours* (1948)
29 Armand Assante, Nastassia Kinski and Dudley Moore in the
re-make of *Unfaithfully Yours* (1984)

a very tender love scene. There would be people listening in the booth and the producer saying, 'Well, it's another way to go, you know', nobody knowing what to say to this famous composer who's written music that is so wrong for the scene. But they never shot this. There was another scene we wrote in which the musicians were gathered to play together in a loft, and the jealousy and suspicion were played out in glances, with the cello played in an accusatory way, and the violin pleading. It was a very delicate scene that was never done, or was turned into a duelling violin number. I think these additions could have made the film worthwhile.

Levinson and Valerie Curtin were divorced in 1982. While making Diner, *he had met Diana Rhodes, a production designer for TV commercials who lived in Baltimore with her son Patrick and daughter Michelle, who played the flower girl at Eddie's wedding. They subsequently married, and though living in a Los Angeles home complete with editing facilities, would also keep a home near Baltimore. They have had two sons – Sam, born in 1985, and Jack, born in 1988, during the shooting of* Rain Man.

Levinson's next film was to be as director only, and was also a literary adaptation. The source material was Bernard Malamud's first novel, The Natural, *written in 1952. Its central character, Roy Hobbs, played by Robert Redford, believes himself to be a great baseball player when young, but his chance to join the big league is ruined when he is shot by a dark temptress, Harriet. Years later, though past his best years, he returns again to fulfil his dream and, despite the forces of time and corruption, is filled with the hope of his childhood sweetheart, Iris.*

After *Diner*, I didn't want to be identified with doing movies that were all going to be like that. I never really wanted to be categorized or have a label. In some quarters people might say I have very little identity as a director, but in terms of being allowed to make films in totally different styles, that's what pleases me.

Robert Redford liked *Diner* a lot, and as a result I went up to Sundance[2] and we spoke there. We flew back to Los Angeles together and he said that maybe we could find an interesting pro-

ject to do together. Time went by, and then I had a meeting with
him about an idea. We talked it over, but he didn't seem too excited about it. Then somehow we began talking about baseball,
since like me he's a real baseball buff. He asked me if I'd read *The
Natural*. In fact, I'd read it years before and had tried to option
it once, but it wasn't available. He said he thought it was available now, and that he had a screenplay. I read the screenplay,
which was by Roger Towne, brother of Robert, and I was kind
of taken with it. The film came together very quickly, and I
didn't do much with Roger's script, as it seemed to me very
workable.

We caught a lot of flak about how we changed the ending. But
in fact we changed the beginning, the middle and the end. In the
book, he of course strikes out at the end, so we were accused of
not being true to the author. I was speaking somewhere and this
came up, so I ran down some of the things that were in the book
and asked whether anyone would have wanted us to film those
scenes. That in a stadium full of 47,000 people, Roy Hobbs fouls
off the ball and it hits Iris in the head and knocks her out. They
stop the game, take her down to the locker room and revive her.
She then tells Roy she's carrying his son. When I asked if anyone
wanted us to film that scene, they all said, 'No, not that one!'
This may have worked in terms of the novel, but what was interesting to me in what Towne did was that the film was not
about a particular baseball game, it was about all the baseball
games that had ever been played. It was like someone telling you
about a catch that someone made – it's not just that he went
back to the wall and caught the ball, it's that they say he went
through the wall! They elaborate the tall tale, and I thought that
was the direction to go with *The Natural*. I don't care about the
reality of it. I love baseball, and if you are a real baseball fan,
you don't talk about yesterday's game but all the games that
went before it, all the stats and details that led up to it. It makes
the particular game you are watching that night all the more
fulfilling.

Although it had a budget five times that of Diner, The Natural
still posed enormous logistical problems in the filming of the

30 Levinson directs his first major star, Robert Redford, in
The Natural (1984)

31 Robert Redford as the ultimate baseball hero Roy Hobbs in *The Natural* (1984)

baseball scenes. The final game was staged in the Buffalo Stadium, known as the War Memorial Stadium, which fortunately for the production team had been recently refurbished.

In the book and the script, the crowds at the games when Hobbs became a big sensation were enormous. And that means if we're shooting towards the pitcher, we'd have to fill all the stands behind him with extras. Then if you want an angle on Hobbs, the same applies – and for each base! So just for a simple sequence, it could mean moving the extras around six or eight times. And then if we're shooting out of continuity, we have to allow for the shifting of the sun. So we had to move the crowds around constantly, which can drive you crazy! The final sequence, in which Hobbs strikes the ball so hard it smashes the stadium clock and sets all the lights off, was shot over a week, restaging it every night to do one more piece. Finally, at five o'clock in the morning, we were blowing up the light towers.

The Natural was shot in seventy-six days, just a week over schedule and slightly over budget. It was to receive an Academy Award nomination for Best Cinematography – the work of Caleb Deschanel, who, along with Levinson, followed through a concept of the film as Arthurian legend. In the opening scenes depicting Hobbs's childhood, Deschanel was inspired by an early two-colour process to emphasize only the pale greens and burnt yellows of the Midwest. This was followed by amber tones in the interiors, and bright, burning sunlight for the daytime baseball games. The stadium scenes were coloured only in black, grey and the deep green of the grass. The women in Hobbs's life were to be sharply differentiated, so that Iris would possess an iridescent quality, while Harriet inhabits shadows and wears only dark clothes. Slow motion was employed at key dramatic moments in Hobbs's games.

I met with Caleb Deschanel because I thought he was the perfect guy to light the film. Up to that time baseball movies[3] had always been very straightforward – like *The Pride of the Yankees*, about Lou Gehrig – all done in a very realistic manner. In my

32 The woman in white, Iris (Glenn Close), in *The Natural* (1984)

33 The dark lady, Harriet (Barbara Hershey), in *The Natural* (1984)

mind, *The Natural* was to be a larger-than-life, mythical, slightly old-fashioned, big-screen, adult fable. No baseball film had really stepped in that direction, and at the time some critics just would not accept that. To me, it was not that serious, but actually rather humorous – but that wasn't the perception of those critics who preferred to see it as a serious piece of work. I had admired Caleb's camerawork on *The Black Stallion*, and I thought he would really work on colour and light in the style I wanted. The Judge in the film always talked about light and dark, so I took off from that. To me, it was a little bit like lighting with a sense of humour. That was the intention, and we stayed committed to that path.

I chose Randy Newman to do the score because I think he has a great sense of Americana. In one of his songs, 'Louisiana', I just hear America. I also thought his sense of irony would work well for the movie. And it turned out that he was a baseball fan too!

It was the first film produced by Tri-Star, and at that point they had a very poor distribution set-up. They wanted to advance our release date so this would be the first Tri-Star film to be seen. We had to race to make this date, and in fact – and this is something I'd never do again – we didn't really finish cutting the film, so it stays in my head for that reason. At the last minute, *Where the Boys Are '84* became the first Tri-Star film released, so we were kicked around for nothing.

If many thought The Natural *an unexpected choice for Levinson, despite its complete immersion in all things authentically American, then his next project was even less predictable.* Young Sherlock Holmes *was a screenplay by up-and-coming writer Chris Columbus (he had previously written* Gremlins*) which had at first attracted the attention of Steven Spielberg, who then offered it to Levinson. Columbus took the Conan Doyle characters of Holmes and Watson, and imagined their first meeting taking place at school, where they uncover a conspiracy involving a house master at the head of an Egyptian religious cult. A series of hallucinations in the film called for the services of George Lucas's special-effects team, Industrial Light and Magic.*

I'm a bad student. I'm not like some directors who can watch movies and then pull out shots and say, 'Gee, I'm going to work off that.' When I finally saw *I Vitelloni*, I realized what Mel Brooks was talking about. But only afterwards can I appreciate the reference point. What I am good at is basically seeing what it is that interests me and being able to pursue that, as opposed to seeing what has been done and then trying to figure out how I would do that. I think today there are two problems among directors – those who are trying to copy and those who are trying to be extremely important. The director's style is coming more and more to the fore, so that you're totally aware of what the director is doing. I prefer to discover the technique only when you watch a film over and over again.

When I watch movies, I watch them like an audience, I don't analyse them. That's probably why I try to make certain camera movements or effects as subtle as possible; I don't like them to be obtrusive. So when I see movies, I just get caught up in them and have no idea how things were done. When you're working in terrain that you know about, there is a tendency for your work to be defined by that area, and I'm looking to stretch that definition, whatever it may be. The benefits of doing something like *Young Sherlock Holmes* are that you have to open up a little bit. You have to explore things you might not otherwise explore, because it's not something that I would write or normally think about doing. And by pushing past those boundaries, when you come back inside them you bring something with you. So it was a very strong learning process.

The nature of working today, compared to the early directors who began with two-reelers in the silent days and then built up to 138 films, is very different, because we can count our films and remember them. I recall King Vidor[4] at a special screening of *The Big Parade* with an orchestra playing and the full works. In the question and answer session afterwards, he was saying, 'Well, I did this film and . . . ' and he paused and said, 'What was the name of that movie?' And I'm thinking, my God, do you actually have to think about that? When in my life am I going to be able to say, 'What was that movie I did?' We simply don't

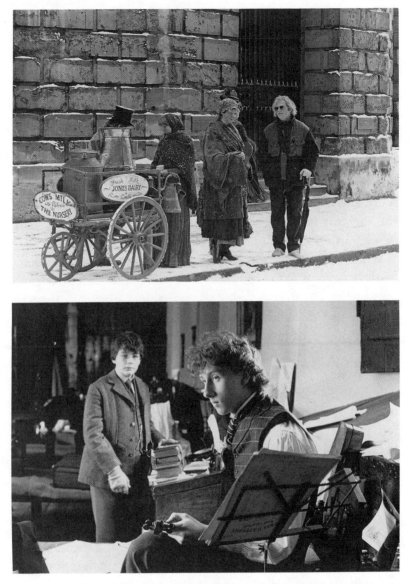

34 Levinson recreates Victorian London in *Young
Sherlock Holmes* (1985)
35 John Watson (Alan Cox) meets Sherlock Holmes (Nicholas
Rowe) in *Young Sherlock Holmes* (1985)

have that learning period. In a way, we have to arrive full-born. I think *Young Sherlock Holmes* gave me a chance to play with some of those tools, which is very beneficial. It was especially helpful to me on *Tin Men*, curiously enough.

I just happened to be reading the script on a vacation, and I was particularly taken by the Victorian aspect of it. I loved the idea that I might have a chance to do a Victorian movie. I like working with kids, though the film was a nightmare to cast: how many sixteen-year-old lead actors are there? I went crazy, looking at 10,000 boys who auditioned on tape. So that part was tough. But the shooting of it was relatively peaceful, and although the boys had no real experience, they were eager to work and easy to get along with.

There were a lot of storyboards on the film, because for continuity's sake you need that kind of work laid out so that you can jump off it and find other routes to accomplish something. In the temple sequences there were so many elements involved that the scenes had to be story-boarded. Of course, if there were people in a room I didn't really need them, because I can work on the blocking there and then. But if part of the temple is burning and one character's running this way, then you need boards.

One of the criticisms faced by the film was that it came out the same year as *Indiana Jones and the Temple of Doom*. It was a mistake on our behalf, because we hadn't seen the Spielberg movie before it opened, and I think we would have been better doing less. The idea was that these misfits from the streets of London had been brought into a cult led by this individual with strong ties to Egypt, because the Egyptians at that time had a great resentment against British colonialism. This individual had a warehouse where he kept this Egyptian cult alive, and the pyramid was meant as a fake, put together as a memento of their past. We would have been better off keeping it as a warehouse with little artefacts rather than trying to make this structure which was way too costly: a phoney, goofy make-believe temple. As soon as audiences saw it, they said, 'This is a real temple?' It was too grand, really. With a warehouse filled with objects catching fire, it would just have been a burning warehouse, and it would have radically changed the visual references for the audience. They would have been less caught up in the grandeur created by that pyramid. It's one of those things you have to watch in production design, and though I think Norman Reynolds did a really good job, in this case I think it was a misinterpretation of what was required. I've learned to work with these elements more carefully, in terms of colour and tone, because certain colours are often not in keeping with what you're doing. And the pyramid was an example of how one small thing can twist a movie slightly beyond what is expected.

Some effects were valid, such as tying the chandelier to the wagon and pulling Holmes out of the fire, because it's almost a mathematical idea. But the sacrifice of the young girl was too much, because of the visual extravagance surrounding it. I think the hallucinations were correct, since you're talking about mind-altering drugs. The vicar confronted by the stained-glass knight doesn't seem to me too bizarre in these terms, and similarly young Watson with the animated food, especially as he was so obsessed with food throughout. I don't have a problem with a mind-altering drug leading people to suicide, so from the attack by the chicken at the very beginning, I would stay with that. If I were to eliminate something, it would not be the flying sequences with the inventor at the beginning, but when Sherlock himself uses the flying apparatus. I would have left it that the professor would have invented flight had he not died, and then it wouldn't have been a distraction; Holmes had been racing across the streets of London in pursuit of the bad guy and ended up down on the ice, so little would have been lost.

The film was shot in about four different castles and in Oxford, all of which made up the school. But predominantly it was a studio movie. I have mixed feelings about studio films. There's a great deal of comfort that comes with shooting in a studio which I'm not sure is always so great. I feel it makes everybody go a little slower, as opposed to freezing your ass off outside, which makes you want to get the work done and gives an energy to it. Also, the real elements are slightly more in keeping with the correct atmosphere, and I think it's more real for the actor. You have to work very hard in a studio to create reality out of an artificial environment, and sometimes that's a struggle. It isn't a case

36 Sacrificial rites inside the pyramid in *Young Sherlock Holmes* (1985)

of, if I can build my sets then let me build them, rather than be on location. The movie will dictate that, because some things just don't exist, as happened on *Bugsy*. In some cases you can build things very quickly and cheaply, put up two walls and knock off a short scene, faking it like that. But I'm not in love with studio film-making. I half prefer the energy of being on location – Thailand, for example – where there are surprises along the way and some of those surprises can be very helpful.

Notes

1   *thirtysomething*, created by the team of Edward Zwick and Marshall Herskowitz, was a successful and influential television series that dealt in serious dramatic terms with the baby-boomer generation. It ran for three seasons from 1988.

2   Located in Provo Canyon, Utah, the Sundance Institute was founded by Robert Redford in 1981 as a cultural centre-cum-workshop where new film talents could be nurtured, especially through script development. Films that owe their life to Sundance include *El Norte* (1983), *Desert Bloom* (1986) and *A Dry White Season* (1990). Held every June in Park City, the Sundance Festival has become famous for discovering new directors – for example, Steven Soderbergh.

3   American cinema has a long tradition of baseball biopics, including James Stewart in *The Stratton Story* (1949), William Bendix in *The Babe Ruth Story* (1948) and Ronald Reagan as Grover Cleveland Alexander in *The Winning Team* (1952), not to mention numerous comedies and musicals.

4   King Vidor (1894–1982) made his feature film début in 1919, and went on to direct over fifty films, including *The Big Parade* (1925), *The Crowd* (1928), *Hallelujah* (1929), *Stella Dallas* (1937) and *The Fountainhead* (1949).

CHAPTER 4

From *Tin Men* to *Rain Man*

Tin Men, written – in fact, dictated to a secretary – in 1985, was Levinson's next Baltimore film after Diner. *Like the earlier film, it delights in the fast dialogue of a group of men – in this case the unscrupulous band of salesmen who conned householders in the early 1960s to have their homes 'improved' by aluminium siding. Two salesmen come into conflict over a traffic accident, and the revenge of the smarter guy – Bill 'B.B.' Babowsky – is to seduce Nora, the wife of the other – Tilley. But as with* Diner, *in doing so both men are made to reassess their relationship with the opposite sex. Also like* Diner, *the film marks the passing of a moment in time, for the tin men are under threat of extinction by a Home Improvement Commission.*

The idea for *Tin Men* came into my head when I was making *Diner*. I was talking to the assistant director, and said, 'If you walk into the diner, all the guys move to the right, and if you go to the left, that's where all the tin men sit.' And I explained that by tin men I meant the older guys. As I said that, I thought, at some point I should really do the story of the tin men. They used to come in and hang around the diner, though sometimes there would be a sign in the window saying, 'No Tin Men Allowed'. To me they were like Damon Runyon characters: they were flamboyant and flashy, and of course they were hustlers and real con-men. I used to sit around the diner while they were telling stories and bullshitting about things. Then my father was sort of in the business – he didn't go out and sell, but the tin men would bring jobs to him to underwrite, and he would pay them off and contract people to do the work. But the tin men drove him crazy, so he gave that up. I knew a fair amount about these guys, and I found it interesting that they were amazingly irresponsible, be-

37 The older but no more responsible 'tin men' in *Tin Men* (1987)

cause when you're younger you assume that guys aged thirty would be very responsible. Basically, they were after enough money to get to the track, and if they got broke, then suddenly they had to canvass and try to pick up more money. That's the way they liked to live their lives – hanging out in clubs, dressing well and being constantly on the hustle.

One day it just occurred to me: what about the coincidence of a guy buying a car, a Cadillac – I love Cadillacs – and another guy having a hassle with his wife, and while distracted by that he bangs his car into this new Cadillac? Then these two guys get into a big fight, and they both find out that the other is a tin man. I found that a good starting point, bringing these two characters together so things would explode and we'd see the rivalry from both sides, and it was really a device to kick off some other themes. Among them would, of course, be the male/female relationship again – one guy having problems with his wife, for reasons explained in the film, the other without any responsibilities, never having lived with someone, and then having to deal with that by taking up with the wife. Sometimes I just get these ideas unexpectedly. One morning I was taking a shower and decided how I could change the whole opening of *Bugsy*.

Although the tin men are older than the characters in *Diner*, they are as emotionally immature as the group that preceded them. So that was an issue to explore; the small things that happen on a daily basis that affect their relationships, and how men often had to make a change in their lives because what they were doing was coming to an end. Hence there would be a conclusion, a sort of end of an era. *Diner* was the end of a decade, and *Tin Men* is basically the end of the next one, even though it's a few years off. So they are companion pieces in more than one way.

The budget for *Tin Men* wasn't really much more than for *Diner*. The difference in its look is mainly because there are more scenes in daylight. Also, the colours in the 1960s were different. *Diner* was five days in wintertime; everyone's wearing overcoats and it's predominantly dark. *Tin Men* was warmer, lighter, and I guess that's a product of the big change in the seasons on the East Coast. But I used the same cameraman, and I had only fifty-two days' shooting, as against forty-two on *Diner*. I suppose it

38 The opening clash between Babowsky (Richard Dreyfuss) and
Tilley (Danny DeVito) in *Tin Men* (1987)

probably is a rather pretty movie, but Peter Sova actually thinks of it as very natural in its look. *Bugsy* is, of course, much more glamorous, because it was the 1940s, and Hollywood then had a very glamorous quality to it. But I think stylistically *Diner* and *Tin Men* are very akin to one another, although *Tin Men* is a much busier, more active film.

I thought of several people to play the lead roles. I've always liked Pacino, and I gave him the script, but he didn't get it. He didn't understand it. Then one day Dreyfuss's name came up, and though I liked him, I couldn't think who could play with him. So I didn't feel right committing to Dreyfuss until I knew who would play the other guy. I couldn't put a combination together in my mind. Then one day I suddenly thought, Danny DeVito, now that would be interesting. I just felt DeVito and Dreyfuss could work as a combination. DeVito had done the TV series *Taxi*, a bit part in *Terms of Endearment* and a lead in Brian De Palma's *Wise Guys*, but that hadn't come out yet. So although I hadn't really seen his work on film, I'd always thought he was a real talent, and I thought he could be an ordinary guy from Baltimore. A lot of actors can't play ordinary guys, because their persona's such that they have to play a character who's larger than life. But I think Richard and Danny can play the common man, so everything then came together very quickly – fortunately for me. Barbara Hershey has always done well since she was young, and again I was looking for an actress who I felt could be living in some other city and wouldn't stand out as being too glamorous.

During the shooting of the movie, I was listening to the first album by Fine Young Cannibals in my trailer. When it came time to deal with the music for the film, we somehow came into contact with their manager, who handed me a cassette, saying, 'Have you heard of these guys, the Fine Young Cannibals?' I said, 'Of course, I've been listening to their music all the time.' He said, 'I just thought you ought to be familiar with them.' I asked if he thought they could actually do a score for me. He felt they could, so we arranged a meeting and talked. I had an idea that they could be on stage in the club scene, which I hadn't yet shot, and then their sound would permeate the whole movie.

39 Babowsky (Richard Dreyfuss) falls in love with Nora
(Barbara Hershey) in *Tin Men* (1987)

That way, some of their vocal music could become score music with slight variations – not orchestrated but very simple. They wrote some songs and I picked out the ones I liked. We shot them on the stage in England, and then integrated that into the film and added in their tracks throughout. Although the film was set in 1963, I didn't feel their sound was radically out of whack. It was more akin to older rock and roll – very simple, a bass guitar, some piano and so on. I gambled that their music would work, and afterwards everybody said, 'Gee, we love these songs. How about an album?' But their company couldn't make a deal with Disney, though several of those songs did make it on to their second album.

When we were preparing *Tin Men*, the production designer kept showing me pictures of houses, but they didn't look right to me. We needed a 'before and after' to show the effect of aluminum siding. I said I wanted a three-storey, wooden-structured house with a little lawn, set back from the road, that probably was in need of a new frame. He kept showing me this stuff and out of frustration I said, 'Do me a favour. Go to 4211 Springdale Avenue, and take a look at that house. It's exactly the kind you should be looking for.' So he comes back and tells me it's perfect. 'It's great,' he says; he wants to show me. And I said, 'I know it's fine, this is *my* house. I didn't say this house, I said a house like this one.' But he insisted it was perfect, so we went to look at it, and I said, 'OK, fine, we'll use it.' This is one of those weird things that happen when you do movies that are very close to an environment you know well. The guy who lets us into the house is the same guy who bought it from my parents. I hadn't been inside this house since the summer of 1963. And inside it's exactly as I remember, because my parents sold it with the furniture. He asks me, 'Would you like to see your old room?' So we go upstairs, and it's the same bedroom that was there when I was a kid. It's like walking back in time – it's exactly the way it was.

So we put period cars on the street, extras walking up and down, and I'm sitting on the porch during a break looking at all this, and it suddenly occurs to me that this is the summer of 1963 when I left. My heart was beating wildly, because I had created exactly what I had seen then; it really was like jumping back in

40 The old Levinson home on Springdale Avenue during the
making of *Tin Men* (1987)

time. A very strange sensation, to be that close to your memories. In a sense, the making of *Tin Men* opened the doors to *Avalon*. The fragments that went together to make *Avalon* had been in my head a long time. So I knew doing *Diner* that I would make *Tin Men*, and now I knew doing *Tin Men* that I would deal with the period before *Diner*, something that would span the generations.

Tin Men *was made under Disney's new production banner, Touchstone Pictures, which counted among its successes such atypical, non-family-type films as* Splash *(1984),* Down and Out in Beverly Hills *(1986) and* The Color of Money *(1986). The budget was a relatively modest $14 million; Levinson brought the film in at $3 million under and it grossed over $30 million, at the same time getting a good critical reception.*

Tin Men was a tough movie, in a sense, though it should have been easy. Because of the tight schedule, and some of the departments being not really up to what they should have been, I found it really draining. It's a constant fight to get certain things done correctly, and if a department is not handling its job well, then you can't always focus on the essentials. So I went from being worn out on *Tin Men* to *Good Morning, Vietnam* in Thailand, where it was 103° and the humidity was about 100. But with all the difficulties shooting in a location like that, it was the easiest thing I've ever done.

Good Morning, Vietnam *was another script brought to Levinson, a real-life story based on the Saigon Armed Forces Radio DJ Adrian Cronauer, who took up his post in 1964. His catchphrase, 'Good morning, Vietnam', lifted from a children's show in Chicago in which Bozo the Clown yelled, 'Good morning, Chicago', introduced a scripted performance with pre-recorded voices – nothing like the improvisations delivered by Robin Williams in the completed film. What was accurate was the way Cronauer fought the army censors and became involved with the Vietnamese – though he left when his tour of duty was over and wasn't kicked out. Ben Moses, co-producer of the film, knew*

Cronauer in Saigon, had stayed in touch, and proposed at first a M*A*S*H-type television series about Vietnam, which was rejected by ABC in 1978. Then a movie treatment was picked up by producer Larry Prezner, who was also the personal manager of Robin Williams. Eventually Jeffrey Katzenberg, chairman of Walt Disney Studios, committed to the project – with Williams attached – for Touchstone Pictures.

Disney had the rights to the script. Mark Johnson showed it to me, I read it and said, 'Well, I'm not crazy about the script, but I like the idea.' What intrigued me was a disc jockey in Vietnam. I liked the idea that Vietnam could be dealt with not from the standpoint of the war, because we know the war in movies – crawling through swamps, crossing rivers with snipers behind you. I mean, some people do that and do it very well, but to be able to talk a little bit about the phenomenon of Vietnam, that was more interesting. I'd never seen the Vietnam War dealt with from the city, from Saigon. I hadn't seen a Vietnam film that showed the Vietnamese as anything but the enemy. I hadn't seen them as people living in a city, working, going to school, just ordinary people. Of course, we were depicting the beginning of the escalation of the war, just before the shit was about to hit the fan. So our intention was simply to give flashes of what was happening – a student riot, or someone being shot by soldiers, in the distance, with traffic going by.

Robin Williams had been attached to the film at Paramount, but they put it in turnaround because they were a little nervous about it. It's funny in retrospect, because now it seems such a commercial project. Before we made it, I talked to some people who went, 'My God, making a film about Vietnam, that's like a death wish.' Of course, this was before *Platoon* and *Full Metal Jacket* had come out. Vietnam was still considered box-office poison, and not only that – I'm doing a comedy! Nobody could envision how you could do anything that's going to be humorous about Vietnam. I think they saw it as some kind of goofy comedy, like Abbott and Costello in Vietnam – a service comedy.

Robin Williams had spent years as a stand-up comedian in nightclubs and in the Comedy Store before landing a guest-starring

41 Adrian Cronauer (Robin Williams) among the Vietnamese in
Good Morning, Vietnam (1987)

role in the TV series Happy Days *as the manic extraterrestrial,*
Mork. After the spin-off series, Mork and Mindy, *Williams*
made his film début in Robert Altman's bizarre 'human cartoon'
musical, Popeye (1980). *In subsequent film appearances, how-*
ever, he had been unable to show the improvisational talents
that were now unleashed in Good Morning, Vietnam.

I thought the idea of this DJ was interesting. The real man was
not as funny as Robin. Not too funny at all. Very serious, in fact.
He wasn't funny in person or on the tapes we listened to. So we
ended up changing about 40 per cent of the script. Working with
Robin on his routines was a little like playing football when we
were kids. We used to say, 'Why don't you go over here? You
there. OK, let's go.' Robin would do a take and I'd say, 'I like
the thing about so-and-so. I don't think that bit works, but this
is good. What about that thing you talked about the other day,
about the nudist monk? Let's give that a try.' Then he'd go and
do another take, we'd go over it again and say, 'This is good,
save this. Drop that. Add this. I think we're in fine shape. Let's
see if you've got any other ideas.' Then another idea would
emerge that wasn't really developed; we'd talk about it and explore it a little more, and then start shooting again. We shot very
fast, a lot of footage, and basically hammered out that whole
section of the movie. We shot it in an incredibly short period of
time considering the impact it has in the movie.

The movie was consciously shot in a pseudo-documentary
style. In the scenes in the booth, the camera is constantly moving
around. I see that on television shows all the time now, a guy's
talking and the camera creeps round him. But we were just looking for a way to do it, to make the film very loose and free-form.
It made sense because we had a lot of Thai and Vietnamese people who made up the classes and so forth, and obviously they
were not actors, so the best thing was to use long lenses and stay
away from them. I wouldn't even put head slates on shots or call
out, so we would just let a scene start with Robin talking, and
everybody did whatever they did and then at some point we
would slate it. Then they would talk again, we'd start shooting
again, and this way the Vietnamese and the Thais had no idea

42 Cronauer (Robin Williams) lets rip over the airwaves in
Good Morning, Vietnam (1987)
43 Levinson directing Robin Williams in his radio monologues in
Good Morning, Vietnam (1987)

when we were actually filming. A lot of it was very improvised in that way, by Robin and also by them, because they were reacting instinctively to what was taking place. That was the best work in the movie, I feel, and that's the way we basically fashioned it.

This was the way the softball game at the end was done. Rather than tell them what they should do, I just let them play softball. They were only given the slightest amount of information about the rules. Then we had two MPs standing there, so I said to them, 'Look, if they get the ball, they're going to run with it. Just keep directing them which way to go, just help them out.' So everyone's running around and I'm the king of the game. Every afternoon we would go out and shoot for about forty minutes, so the actual game spanned four or five days.

What little political reaction there was to the film was very good. I spoke to a number of veterans who felt it said a lot without actually showing the fighting. I think that because there was humour in the film, and no graphic violence, the political implications were probably overlooked by some, who just considered it a diversion.

A lot of people thought I was making a horrendous mistake to do a movie of this sort. I guess it was sort of dangerous, because you know you're only going to make x number of movies, and if you get a shot at making a movie, then you figure what the hell, make the movie you're going to make. You can't try and work out what's supposed to do well or not do well, or plan your career on how well you're going to be received, or how acclaimed you may be. My feeling is that you go with whatever you are interested in, and let that be the guide.

All the movies I had made until then had done good business, none of them had been box-office flops, but all of a sudden *Good Morning, Vietnam* was a mega-hit. It does $130 million and then it goes over 200, and then sells several million cassettes. So now I'm a big commercial union director, whereas before I was labelled as a kind of fringe director. That's the way the business functions: suddenly you've found the key to the audience, and all the bullshit that follows. It's funny and strange.

Rain Man *proved to be another unpredictable success story, beginning also from an unpromising script that had been worked on by Barry Morrow, Ron Bass and Richard Price. Tom Cruise and Dustin Hoffman had, however, remained committed to the project, which dealt with an ambitious, self-centred young salesman, Charlie Babbitt, discovering that all his father's inheritance had been given to a high-functioning autistic brother, Raymond, of whose existence he didn't know. The story followed Charlie as he drives Raymond across the States in an attempt to secure the family fortune and finds himself having to question his old values as some kind of relationship between the brothers develops.*

I had seen the script of *Rain Man* when I was in post-production on *Tin Men*, and I had passed on it. I was too busy on *Tin Men* really to give it any thought; it had been around a long time and everybody was having problems with it. First it was with Marty Brest, then Steven Spielberg, and then Sydney Pollack. Mike Ovitz asked me if I could help out Sydney, as I had tried to with *Tootsie*, because he was really struggling with it. I read the script, and the next day I drove my wife Diana, her sister and her brother-in-law to Palm Springs. As we headed out of Los Angeles across the desert, I explained the story to Diana. Then we went past the windmills, and I'm saying, 'Those windmills would be great for the picture.' When we get to the hotel, Diana says that this is a terrific story and I should direct the movie. I said, 'Diana, I'm just reading it to pass my ideas on to Sydney Pollack. He's going to do the movie.' But she keeps insisting I should do it, and I'm getting a little angry. For the next three days she keeps talking about the script and other ideas go on occurring to me, but I keep saying, 'I'm not doing this movie. Sydney Pollack's going to do it, and he starts shooting in about ten weeks.'

Suddenly one day Ovitz calls me. 'What do you want to do? Sydney Pollack has just dropped out of *Rain Man*. He just wasn't comfortable with it, couldn't resolve certain problems,' he said. 'I know you're interested. Do you want to do it?' So I said, 'Let's see if we can make it work.' It was now seven weeks

44 Charlie Babbitt (Tom Cruise) discovers his forgotten brother
Raymond (Dustin Hoffman) in *Rain Man* (1988)

from principal photography and we had to figure out everything, because Sydney had Arizona and I didn't like Arizona; I didn't think Los Angeles to Arizona was enough of a trip. I felt it should start somewhere in the East, and because some years ago I had stopped in Cincinnati, I thought, what about Cincinnati? It's got rolling hills and a river and bridges, so I told the production designer to take a look, and then all of a sudden we began actively to pursue this movie.

Levinson found it necessary to make a considerable number of changes to the script, which, it seems, was an impossibly colourful road movie with the two central characters getting into dangerous situations, including a brush with the Mafia. In addition, there were problems with the question of communication between the autistic Raymond and his brother, to whom he was originally prone to deliver such clumsily explicit aphorisms as, 'Think about yourself, Charlie Babbitt.'

The writers' strike came about three weeks before principal photography, but it didn't have much bearing on the script as most of the changes we made were done while we were out on the road. All the problems that the previous directors had had with the script came, in a sense, from the ways they were trying to approach it. Whereas the problems I had were, I thought, easily correctable. Basically, I threw out all the events that were taking place on the road, so as not to make it about the obstacles and the dangers they faced. Originally, there was an encounter with a motorcycle gang, and Raymond was able to build a motorcycle for them to escape on! Then in Las Vegas they got into trouble with a hooker, were sent to jail, but Raymond knew all about the law and managed to secure their release. And so on. I thought, if we could keep it to two people, and the problems Charlie has in dealing with Raymond – the exhausting amount of time and commitment necessary to deal with that kind of behaviour – that would basically be the piece. Then we could find the humour inherent in that, not as an extraneous thing but more as an internal problem between two people.

I felt it was necessary to have a scene where they would intend to fly but then couldn't because of Raymond, as otherwise I didn't understand why they would drive across country over such a distance. I remembered the fact that Quantas had never crashed, a piece of useless information that suddenly came in handy, so I used that as an interesting way to launch them on the road. So now Charlie's got real problems, because he said he'd be there in three hours, and because of Raymond it's going to take him three days. Then there's the device of 'Who's on first?' – the absurd Abbott and Costello routine – showing that Raymond didn't understand comedy, that he had no sense of humour. That seemed to me thematic to the piece, as it was a comedy routine which is a struggle of communication in itself. At one point I had Charlie trying to explain the joke, because I liked the idea of taking a routine and playing it without humour.

I used this as a kind of thread throughout the movie, especially in moments of anxiety, such as the car-crash scene, so you saw how committed Raymond was to something, how immovable he was in not going back on the road because it frightened him. To have him walking along the road in front of the car, doing 'Who's on first?' all the way along, that would reveal how much of a prisoner Charlie has become: this is the way Raymond functions and there is no escaping him. This was carried through into the following scene, when Raymond insists on staying in the motel and not going outside as it's raining, with the jump cuts showing that Charlie's stuck there in the room with him all day long. With his realization that Raymond can draw the carpet exactly and answer all the questions on a quiz show – even though many of these things sail over Charlie's head – we could pick up all these details about Raymond along the way.

Dustin Hoffman had done extensive research into autism, and he felt very committed to trying to portray an autistic correctly. I agreed with him, and that's why in a sense the film evolved into more about that, rather than a series of dramatic events. So the smallest details became more important. It was a very loose way of working; we were finding a lot of things to try all the time, and that was also what was so much fun about doing it. Most movies that deal with a disease or whatever try to find a way to cure the individual, but *Rain Man* doesn't do that at all. It says,

45 Raymond (Dustin Hoffman) refuses to fly in *Rain Man* (1988)
46 Charlie (Tom Cruise) and Raymond (Dustin Hoffman) trapped
in their motel room in *Rain Man* (1988)

here's a guy, this is his problem, but we're not going to change or correct him, we are not even going to cure him. There's nothing clinical about the piece at all. For me, the movie was different in that it was about two people on the road. One has a problem and we're saying, 'OK, that's the way it is.' So we would build a montage of the way he sees the road. Our research showed that one particular autistic loved to take photographs, so we had Raymond taking pictures all the time as they go across country – this was something that emerged as we began shooting.

I wanted to start in the present in order for these two guys to have to come to terms with themselves, and discover if there was something in their past that had happened in order to place them where they were now. So I thought, if there was this 1949 Buick which their father had loved and they both loved, if they took this car across country, then it would all seem like we're *in* the past, because that's part of the journey that they have to make to rediscover their past. Then, as they emerge from that, they would come into Las Vegas, and all of a sudden we are back in the modern world.

One day during shooting I said to Dustin and Tom, 'I think we need a little scene, because the audience may assume that it's one thing for Charlie not to show any great affection for Raymond in the early part of the movie, but at least he should make some kind of slight overture to him.' It occurred to me that if Raymond had only one set of clothing, then Charlie could give him some fresh underwear and acknowledge his existence with that. Then I thought Raymond would have a problem with different underwear, so it developed into the whole thing about his getting his underwear from K-Mart in Cincinnati.

I found Dustin very easy to work with. He has ideas, and some of them are terrific and others you go, 'No, I don't see it that way', or maybe that will kick off another idea and something else will emerge. I think that's all you can expect of an actor. If an actor wants everything to be the way he wants it to be, then it's best to say, 'Look, get your own fucking movie and do it yourself.' But if you are working in a collaboration, that's terrific, because if you are exchanging ideas you may find a better one that

47 Charlie (Tom Cruise) and Raymond (Dustin Hoffman) make
contact in Las Vegas in *Rain Man* (1988)

48 Dustin Hoffman being directed by Levinson in *Rain Man* (1988)

takes you to a higher level. That's what gives you adrenalin; it's what drives you and stimulates you.

I thought Tom Cruise did well, because he had to drive the whole movie. He had to be on top of it the whole time, because if he didn't the movie would lay down. You're always looking for the arc of the character, and in the case of *Rain Man*, in the traditional story sense, the revelations are in the arc of Cruise's character, because Raymond is not going to have one. He is just in his own world, and if there was no conflict with that, he would have been very content to stay in that motel for ever, as long as he gets the things he needs. That's what I mean by the Cruise character having to push the movie.

A number of actresses were considered for the role of his girl-friend. In the script, she had the line, 'Don't you understand, Charlie, you've kidnapped him.' I always found that line to be amazingly melodramatic, and yet it was valid, because he did kidnap Raymond and it launches the movie. But I didn't know how it could be said, so I suggested casting a foreign actress, be-cause then the line would take on a different tone. Also, a foreigner wouldn't understand things as well, and since she's a little bit in the dark, her lines wouldn't be quite as on the nose as with an American actress. I also felt that since this movie was about lack of communication, no one would understand anyone else: an Italian wouldn't understand Charlie that well, Charlie didn't understand his brother, and Raymond didn't understand anybody. So an accent would take the edge off the melodramatic scenes and, in my mind, make it more acceptable. She could sit in the car at the Institute waiting for them because she wouldn't know what the hell Charlie was talking about. Whereas an American actress would say, 'What do you mean? Why should I be at the end of a driveway? What's at the end of the driveway?' It would have needed very different dialogue.

I wasn't going to appear in the movie originally. J. T. Walsh was cast as the doctor, but he was caught up in a movie and wasn't available. Dustin kept saying, 'Well, you should do it.' I said, 'Please, I don't want to have to go through that.' But he said I should, because I understood the movie. Until the night before I was trying to find somebody, but I couldn't, so I said, 'All right,

49 Raymond (Dustin Hoffman) and Charlie (Tom Cruise) strike out
together in *Rain Man* (1988)
50 The foreign Susanna (Valeria Golino) following her boyfriend
Charlie (Tom Cruise) in *Rain Man* (1988)

I'll try it. I'll look at the dailies and, if it's OK, we'll go ahead. Otherwise we'll have to kill that day and find another actor.' I got by with it because I knew how to push the piece a little bit and improvise, so it was just like a director trying to find extra moments. I was concerned not to make him very doctorish and patronizing, but more matter-of-fact, with at least a hint of humanity.

Given how easy it might have been to emphasize the melodramatic side to the film, there were two things I wanted to avoid in the music: no shit-kicking guitar music when we were on the road, and no strings to add to the emotional scenes. I was listening to the song 'Scatterlings of Africa' and I loved its rhythm, so ultimately that turned up as they were going across Palm Springs, with the big windmills all around. And with that I decided that this rhythmic style of music was the way I wanted to go. So I talked it over with my composer, Hans Zimmer, in England, and that's what we had, this very odd kind of rhythm. Very unlike what you'd expect with this type of movie, but it made sense for me.

Nobody thought the movie was going to make any money. I felt that having made one film that happened to do very well, this would be a kind of offbeat piece, even if it did star Tom Cruise. On opening night, I drove past one of the theatres and it was half full. So I thought, it's going to do some business, but not do particularly well. Then all of a sudden it has a respectable weekend figure, gets bigger the next week and just keeps getting bigger. I thought the whole idea of autism would have kept a lot of people away. At that time MGM/UA was not a healthy studio, and we had only one preview. We never showed the cards to the studio – they were really mediocre. The audience resented the fact we didn't have a happy ending. One person even told me, 'I thought the little guy was going to snap out of it at the end!' And they thought Charlie was too cruel to his brother, that we should have made him nicer. But I didn't want to pander to the audience like that; I felt the ending was correct for the movie, and that I was right to go on my own feelings about the piece. I certainly didn't set out to make something that was going to be this great piece of mass entertainment.

51 Levinson plays the doctor in the closing scenes of
Rain Man (1988)

Rain Man *was nominated for eight Academy Awards, and went on to win five, including Best Film and Best Director for Levinson. It also won the Golden Bear as the Best Film at the 39th Berlin International Film Festival in 1989, and Levinson received the Best Director award from the Directors' Guild. After coming in under budget by $2.5 million, it has gone on to gross an estimated $500 million.*

CHAPTER 5

Avalon

With the huge commercial success of Good Morning, Vietnam *and* Rain Man, *Levinson could safely be described as the hottest director in Hollywood, though neither film had been made with such great expectations. His evident skill in handling 'difficult' actors – Redford, Hoffman – had shown that he could probably turn his hand to anything, starring anybody, and the studios began to court him. By forming his own company, Baltimore Pictures, along with regular producer Mark Johnson, he secured a deal with Tri-Star to make films without any studio interference. Inspired by one line that kept recurring in his head – 'If I knew that things would no longer be, then I would have tried to remember them better' – he began to research the idea of putting on film the history of his family. This was clearly not going to be a mainstream movie, nor a genre that any studio might commonly feel comfortable with.*

I often feel a bit like a salmon going upstream, fighting the tendency to want a shorthand – what's it all about, tell us quickly. When you do movies that don't give you a story right away, there's a danger of the audience's brains going to sleep, because they may not have any interest other than getting right into it. Television has basically accentuated this, because any drama has to go boom before that first commercial break; they've got to suck you into the piece and hold you, whatever device they may use. Even if it's a lousy story, even if it's been told fifty times in fifty different ways, that's what many gravitate to. I mean, Dickens is a great storyteller, but I don't know if that kind of storytelling applies very well to the American movie-goer today, because Dickens brings a complexity well beyond what most audiences want. There are too many characters, too many different kinds of stories. Say, there's a drug problem – well, that's a story. The requirement is not in terms of real story structure, but give them a big arcade game and then they understand it. That's basically what *Terminator 2* is all about – it's an arcade game. You know there's a problem, and things keep shooting and clanging and ricocheting and banging, so that even if the work's been done well, it's still an arcade film to me. When you don't give an audience a clear design right away on what you're doing, there's a great impatience, and frequently a lack of interpretation. So even if I have a scene where a character is lying, the real lying comes off as the truth, because you've got to tell it well enough for another character to believe it. But sometimes when you create ambiguities in terms of one character saying one thing and doing something else, there's a danger the audience will take it at face value. There's very often no real interpretive thinking going on. All of these things make it more difficult for film-makers in today's world. If audiences are more passive, letting themselves drift off, it makes it much harder for character-driven work.

I was criticized on *Avalon* for spending too much money on a personal movie. Like, a personal movie should be $1 million, and real commercial exploitation can be $40 million. It isn't my fault that a movie costs $22 million. We had a lot of actors, but they didn't cost a great deal, and I took one-third of what I would normally get. But to deal with a period piece sweeps up a lot of time, and in contemporary America that's going to cost $22 million. I had no control over that. We shot the movie in sixty-four days, which is a very modest shoot considering the number of characters and the different time periods.

No studio basically wants to make a movie that's personal and doesn't have some gimmick. Not that they don't do them periodically, just that they'd rather not. They'd much rather have something closer to *Robocop*. They go, 'Yes, he's a cop but he's a machine, lots of shooting and explosions. We know that material if we do it well.' And I have to sympathize with the dilemma. If you do make an exploitation type of film and you don't really do it well, then you may succeed only at 60 per cent of what you want out there. But you can still succeed in terms of box office.

If you make a more personal movie and you miss what you intend to do by 15 per cent, then the failure rate is much greater. You don't have the same leeway if you make a movie that is personal and character-driven as you do with the bigger pieces of arcade-orientated work. If Woody Allen misses by a little bit, then that's it.

In the case of *Avalon*, the studio never said it, but I know they would have preferred me to come in with something else. And they were never comfortable with it in terms of the way they distributed it. I think even if the studio executives talked about it, they really didn't do the job they should have done. It went out with such a big break, so fast, that it was like throwing the movie to the wind. Originally we opened in six theatres and did very well. The next week we went up 6 per cent, which was great. So then it should have gone to thirty, then fifty, then at least 150 theatres, so that it would have been nurtured. Instead of which they went from six theatres to 600, and the movie couldn't handle it that quickly. Clearly at the beginning there was good word of mouth, but word of mouth can't spread as fast as going from six to 600. It should have been released with a lot less speed.

The idea for *Avalon* came from when I was in Baltimore scouting locations for *Tin Men*. I was walking around off a street called Broadway, and I suddenly looked round and something was very familiar to me. I realized that my grandfather used to have a wallpaper store around the corner, and there was another building which was originally a movie theatre I used to visit when I was very little. But I couldn't remember it all that well, and I thought, if I knew that things would no longer be, then I would have tried to remember them better. This stood out in my mind, the idea that we never realize how things are not going to stay for ever, that the neighbourhood you grow up in may one day be totally gone. Only these half-images will remain.

The idea developed as I spent more time in Baltimore, and I began to think more thematically: That once upon a time there was a big town and that gradually the family drifted away. I remembered how my father became involved in a client's business in television, and how we moved to suburbia because we actually did better as a result. So I thought, well, television, and

52 Irv Levinson at the Appleton Street family home in *Avalon* (1990)

how the rise of television, together with the break-up of the American family, was an interesting theme to play with. Families sitting round the television eating their dinners, rather than at the table. It all began to click when I'd finished *Rain Man*, and then it poured out.

Levinson returned to Baltimore to interview his relatives for source material. Many of his discoveries were to be worked into the script, such as the hitherto unknown fact that his grandfather once owned a black night-club, and how breaks with family traditions led to relatives refusing to speak again to each other. The film opens in 1914 with the grandfather, Sam Krichinsky, arriving in Baltimore during a Fourth of July celebration, then interweaves Sam's stories of the past with the trials of the next generation and their building up of the discount business to the point where their uninsured warehouse goes up in flames. As the film progresses, the family splinters and the old values are replaced by new ones. Where public holidays were once a time of celebration and family gatherings, now they become excuses for commercial exploitation.

The film draws on my family from my mother's side. The Levinson side, my father's side, was a very small family, there were very few of them. So the Krichinskys were the larger side, with five brothers, and most of my family remembrances revolved around that side because there were all these cousins, whereas there were no other Levinson kids. My grandfather was in the wallpaper business, my father was in the appliance business, so all these elements began to mesh.

My grandfather used to tell stories. So it was the storyteller colliding with the universal storyteller, television, which would win at the end. I remember the television arriving in the house all gift-wrapped, and then years later visiting my grandfather, who was sitting alone with a television on in the background. In the final scene there's the grandfather, who starts to talk again about when he came to America, and his grandson's child is watching a parade with balloons on television, and he's giving his attention to the screen rather than the storyteller. All this

53 The Krichinsky brothers assembled at a hospital in *Avalon* (1990)

made sense, and at the same time I would be taking these simple family problems throughout the years as my subject.

I'm from the generation that straddled these two, and the next generation has only the television storyteller, and has evolved from what television has done in changing our perceptions and the way we act. Obviously, I wasn't going to get all this into one movie, but the theme of these two influences criss-crossing one another was what I wanted to show. I liked the idea that although in the end Jules gave up selling televisions when the store went under, he went on to sell airtime for commercials, so he became the ultimate slave to the device.

I think much greater conning goes on in television than from any salesman. A salesman can only knock on so many doors a day. If 35 million people watch a sales pitch on television at any given moment, then I think it is affecting us in ways that I don't know that anyone has even begun to consider. I don't know how you can evaluate it. All I know is, somebody watches television and assumes that what they see, they can have. That's what the message is: 'You can have this.' It doesn't say you have to work to get it. If you have the plastic, you can have this, you can go there. It has nothing to do with any sense of ethics, period. There's no residual morality either. If you think of the thousands of hours of commercials that we watch, well, that's the selling of America. I think an amazingly perverted sensibility comes out of it. I've watched people in shopping malls. They're all wandering around, but how many people actually want something? Or are they there because they think they want something? Do they really need it? Are they there because this message keeps getting to them? This is probably symptomatic of where television has brought us: thousands, millions of people wandering aimlessly through shopping malls at all times, shopping.

There is no area called Avalon. Although I did see somewhere in a newspaper the claim that there was, even though I had denied it existed in Baltimore. But I'd never heard of the place that was mentioned. Avalon just came to me one day. There was an Avalon movie theatre in Baltimore that we used to go to a lot. I also thought it was interesting in terms of King Arthur, that there was this mythical place, an earthly paradise. It was ap-

54 Sam Krichinsky (Armin Mueller-Stahl) as the storyteller
in *Avalon* (1990)
55 Three generations of Krichinskys gather round the television set
in *Avalon* (1990)

propriate given that the family was getting further and further away from Avalon, and losing something very special. You don't know if it's the house, or if it's the neighbourhood. When Gabriel says, 'When we were in Avalon, nobody ate!' you get the sense that even though they were poor, there was something about the time and place in terms of family that was very important. I thought of Baltimore as an English city, because it was founded as an English colony, with Queen Mary giving the name to Maryland. So Avalon made sense to me in that way – perhaps something English, but something that's lost.

The immigrant experience in terms of the sweatshop and tenements and the teaming masses, that didn't apply to Baltimore in the same way. Of all the stories that I've ever heard, that kind of struggle didn't occur. Not that they weren't poor and didn't have to carry ice up to some place, and so on. But it wasn't like New York. My relatives used to talk about living on Jackson Place, which I guess is one of the earlier places that families used to live in the centre. The houses would be almost in a quad, with a centre area of grass and fountains. If you applied that to New York, you'd know damn well that no immigrants were living in those conditions. And that's one of the first areas that they lived in Baltimore. My family came to Baltimore because the first brother came here and got a job in a department store. I mean, they wouldn't even have thought about New York. Baltimore – that's where they were going. They didn't all go through New York. The immigrant experience was very varied. That was one of the things I wanted to put in the film, even though the movie is not just about that, or I would have spent more than seven minutes on it. Even then, it's told through a storyteller, so everything is larger than life, what with the fireworks exploding – who knows if they really saw fireworks or anything like that? But if you're telling the story, it's got to be a good story. That, I think, is the joy of the storyteller.

At the beginning of the film, I was trying to find a style that would be slightly unrealistic, because it's told through the mind's eye. I thought it ought to look different from the rest of the movie, because whether it's true or not is something we're never going to know. I thought about black and white, but then I real-

56 Arriving in Baltimore on the 4th of July in *Avalon* (1990)

ized MTV has used black and white too much; they've used it up. Then I thought of desaturation, but that would give the brown-and-white look of *The Godfather*, and I didn't want that absence of tones. Then Allen Daviau[1] came in one day and said, 'What about shooting at 16 frames per second and printing at 24, doubling every other frame?' So I said, 'Let's take a look at it, and we did it several different ways, and when I saw the 16/24 effect I thought, this is really interesting. We worked on a kind of filtration for it, and came up with a design that doesn't seem quite real, but you don't know exactly what it is. I suppose it approaches newsreel, if anything. It's a little like old-time movies, except they pixillate and kind of dance around, and this wasn't doing that. So it does seem off, and I don't think anyone can quite figure it out.

I chose Allen Daviau as the cinematographer because I liked his work on *Empire of the Sun*. I particularly liked the opening scenes in Shanghai in terms of the colours and tones; I didn't want *Avalon* to be too bright, and yet I didn't want to avoid colours. I wanted reds, but not a strong Technicolor look. So we spent a lot of time finding a way of arriving at that, and I think he did a very accomplished job.

On *Avalon*, as on all my movies since *Diner*, I used multiple cameras. On *Diner*, it was really an accident. We were on a forty-two-day shooting schedule, and thirty-one of those were nights and harder to shoot. Because of an electrical fire we lost one night, so we explained to MGM that we'd be a day over, and they said no, we couldn't have another day. I had said I was going to make it in forty-two days, so that's what I was supposed to do. They were very nice about that, just as they were about the whole movie! I couldn't figure out how to shoot all this stuff that we had to do to make up for that lost day. Then Peter pointed out that since we were carrying an extra camera, why not use two cameras some of the time? So we put two cameras into position, with one on a single and one on a two-shot, or sometimes two different angles on the two-shot. We started doing a scene this way and the sound guy said, 'Well, you know, one of the guys off-camera is overlapping.' And I said, 'What does that mean?' I really didn't know any better then. He ex-

57 Levinson and cinematographer Allen Daviau discuss a shot
in *Avalon* (1990)

plained that the off-camera people would be stuck, with only the on-camera tracks usable. So I said, 'Why don't we put mikes on the people off-camera so we hear them as good as the others?' I didn't know how to make the overlaps work when there was a different rhythm to the scene. So we now had two cameras, and microphones on everybody, and that technique became very important, because if I had a good take, then I had at least two camera set-ups and all the dialogue with overlaps. In some cases I couldn't cover as much as I might have, and in the finished movie certain lines which came out really funny and were an overlap are off-camera, and I never did get it the same when I came around for the change of angle. But at least I heard it!

Of course, if you're doing a shot that's more involved, then two cameras are not going to be that useful, but then that extra camera can be used to shoot something else for the movie without the principals. So with two cameras, I've found it to be a much faster way to work. Ultimately, if you've got the performance you want, then you've got it in several angles, which is very beneficial for the type of work I'm doing, which is much more relationship-orientated. Unless I'm limited to the use of one camera because of the design, I'm going to be in there with a second camera. I don't think we have ever decided to sacrifice the real look of a movie as a result, and, obviously, if you want to do dinner scenes you would use two cameras so that everybody can talk. To me the dinner conversations in *Avalon* are very realistic, with people overlapping one another, and the reactions of people turning from one to another, and when you are getting spontaneity and can shoot it several ways at one time, it makes a huge difference. If you have planned sixteen set-ups, then because of the way you are covering it, it's actually going to be thirty-two. So you can say to yourself, well, I got it in this shot, and when she reacted over there at the same time, I have that too. That moment was so great, she was hearing the line for the first time, and she really laughed! We didn't need to shoot a lot of takes on *Avalon* – five at the most.

I used much less source music in *Avalon* than I would normally. Just a few Al Jolson things. It didn't seem correct, because the movie needed to flow a little bit – as we were running in and

58 Two cameras lined up on the set of *Rain Man* (1988)

59 A family meal scene in *Avalon* (1990)

out of different time periods, backwards and forwards – and there was a tendency to jump time: a man walks into a room, sits in the chair, the light grows dim, and then he gets up and in the same shot he's become an old man. Ten years have passed. So I didn't want to bang out some kind of Beatles song to emphasize the point – the television is just playing something else, which was *My Favorite Martian*. The same for the screen doors as we're getting further and further away from Avalon. Baltimore is full of these screen doors, so suddenly you cut to this surburban scene on the screen door and the next thing you know, we're inside a house. I wanted the music to be like that, have a more lyrical function and not punctuate time too much.

I had been listening to Randy Newman's album *Land of Dreams*, and I thought that was a good sound picture for *Avalon*. I didn't have to think twice about it – the second I heard it, I thought, oh yes, that's what it should be like. Randy responded to my script and it went from there. Generally, he would compose after the fact. In this case, with the waltz at the very beginning of the movie, we were somewhere into the middle of the shoot and I called him up. I said, 'Randy, I need some waltz music for the scene when they're getting married, something for them to dance to.' I asked him if he could just knock something out on the piano that we could use as a temporary track, and that became the main theme. He sent it to me and I loved it, thought it was great. He put three other numbers on the tape, so when we began to rough-cut the movie, I ended up putting these against the film in other places. In that way the music was fixed early on, which made Randy complain that I'd made things harder for him! I played the music a lot on the set while we were shooting because it seemed to suggest the rhythms of what was taking place, as well as giving us the mood of it all. Then the old man had to play the theme on the piano, so now that piece of music had to be in the movie as well.

Levinson was nominated for an Academy Award for Best Original Screenplay for Avalon. *If the film did not achieve the success Levinson might have wished, then this remains the problem faced by any director wishing to make a film that is contempla-*

tive and complex, rather than fast and dumb. If he avoids deep discussion of psychological issues, Levinson is more than often animated on social questions, and this is where he hopes a film like Avalon will make its mark. His films have been criticized for an element of conservatism, but it is really more a question of maintaining basic human standards. Levinson has cited a recent survey which shows that, faced with a multiple choice exam, 50 per cent of American high-school students couldn't identify North America on a map and 33 per cent thought Adolf Hitler was a German soccer coach. This kind of ignorance, alongside the rise of greed as a motivating force in the corporate USA of the 1980s, is what angers Levinson most.

Pauline Kael said that in *Avalon*, just as in *The Natural*, I took a Republican view of life in terms of the family, though she conceded that the character of Ann didn't fit the thesis. I don't know how I could have a character in my script disagreeing with such views that *I* didn't create. It's an absurd statement on her part. I didn't subscribe to Reagan's politics nor to the politics of the Republicans in any one way you can point to. Everything about the Reagan administration was a lie, so to be seen as part of Reagan's view of America is a label that I find irritating. But in some ways I'm not bothered by this kind of criticism, because if I make a movie and that's all you can think and talk about, then in a sense I've done my job. If you see a movie and it's like two hours in a vacuum – nothing lingers and you just go on with your life – then I'd be worried. But if you're writing movies in which things are just a little complicated, whether the reaction is negative or positive, at least there's something to talk about. I think my films are open to a lot of interpretation, and misinterpretation. I don't think anybody sees a movie and thinks, well, from now on I'm going to be a good neighbour. Frank Capra talked about showing what American society was and what it was capable of, how the little man could take on the system, the human spirit and all that stuff. But I'm not sure anyone took that as a cue to better mankind, and I don't know if the cinema can do that.

What worries me is that with the demise of literature, the band of what seems acceptable is becoming narrower and narrower. It's as if now you can make movies with a loud bass, because even if you're not that crazy about the material, at least there is this bass playing along to keep you going, to excite you. It's like the effect of rock on MTV, where there's a bass driving and multi-images that keep going faster – let's fast-forward, get to the exciting bits! I think that's why we are less capable of handling foreign films than we were, and I don't just mean French cinema. Those British films of the 1930s and 1940s with actors like Leslie Howard or Charles Laughton are becoming culturally more isolated as well. The way the British speak sounds too different; we have less of a tolerance for it – a generation just shuts off.

I think the death of Broadway is a warning to cinema. There may be a *Phantom of the Opera* or a *Les Miserables*, but what happened to all that other work that used to be on Broadway? We all know the economic problems of the movie business, but without the vitality of individual voices the business will die. If a director is simply making a movie that the studio wants, then in a sense that becomes the death of the business. Along the line somebody has to come up and say, 'I have a great idea', and they should make that movie and not be led by a group. If I'm hungry for a hamburger, I may ask myself, should I go to this place I've never heard of, Harry's Hamburger? Now, McDonald's, I know about. But if I go there I will have only a McDonald's hamburger, and I might be missing the surprise of discovering that Harry's is the greatest hamburger stand along Route whatever it is. We've got to be prepared to be surprised along the way, and disappointed along the way. If we can't have that in the marketplace, then it's over.

Levinson is, of course, not the only film director to have put Baltimore on the cinematic map. One-time underground cult figure John Waters has also remained faithful to his native city, from his early outrageous, low-budget quickies such as Pink Flamingos *(1978) to the more recent camp social satires,* Hairspray *(1988), about a teen dance program in 1962 Baltimore and* Cry Baby *(1990).*

We're from different sides of town, which is why we are so different. Baltimore is very much a neighbourhood-orientated city, and his was another neighbourhood, but I understand the Eastern Avenue characters he uses and how he has arrived at that burlesque style.

Notes

1 Allen Daviau's other credits as cinematographer include *E. T.* (1982), *The Falcon and the Snowman* (1985) and *The Color Purple* (1986). He was nominated for Academy Awards for his work with Steven Spielberg and for *Avalon*.

CHAPTER 6

From *Bugsy* to *Toys*

Once a street-smart Brooklyn hoodlum, Benjamin 'Bugsy' Siegel rose in the crime world to form a partnership with Meyer Lansky. Along with 'Lucky' Luciano, they took control of the New York underworld after bootlegging during Prohibition. From 1931 they masterminded the Mafia's move into gambling – first in Cuba and then in Nevada, the first state to legalize casinos. Established as a ruthless killer by his leadership of the underworld assassination squad, Murder Incorporated, Bugsy also had enormous charm, which he put to great effect when he arrived in California in the late 1930s. He established various gambling operations and, through his friendship with actor George Raft, infiltrated the Hollywood set. Siegel continued to kill; among his victims was his old buddy-turned-informer Harry Greenberg in 1938. After discovering Las Vegas, a modest town with a few casinos, in 1945, he bought a piece of desert 7 miles out of town and began to build the Flamingo, at an initial estimated cost of $1 million. As the figure soared towards $6 million, Siegel announced a grand opening over Christmas 1946. It was a disaster, with few of the promised Hollywood stars turning up. A reopening in March 1947 fared little better. On 20 June that year, Siegel was shot dead in the home of his girlfriend, Virginia Hill. It is believed that this was the work of Lansky and his associates, who had been helping with Siegel's debts but suspected him of secretly putting money aside with Hill in a Swiss bank account. Lansky continued to build up Las Vegas, making it the gambling capital it is today.

Bugsy *was a long-term obsession of Warren Beatty, who had commissioned James Toback to write the script back in 1984. In the event Toback was six years late in delivering the script, which he had hoped to direct himself. However, Toback's track*

record was nothing like as secure as Levinson's – since his bi-
zarre and violent début film Fingers *(1978), none of his films had*
met with any success. Beatty's theory was that three intelligences
were better than two in making a movie, and since he liked
Levinson's way with actors (he had at one time been approached
for Tin Men*), he brought in the director who had previously*
professed a lack of interest in crime thrillers.

I came on *Bugsy* when Warren showed me the script. It was
about 250 pages, and I thought, this is interesting, there's some
great work in here and I think it could be a great movie. I didn't
want to spend more time developing the script. Instead I said,
'Well, let's go ahead and commit to shooting this movie.' I could
assume that we would be intelligent enough to make the changes
that had to be done between then and the start of principal photography. And Warren was more than willing, as was Toback,
so we began to move ahead.

I think the script we had was not as close to a final version as
Roger Towne's had been on *The Natural*, but from reading Toback's work you had to be an idiot not to realize its potential.
I think he's an exceptional writer; he creates great dialogue and
interesting scenes. So I could say, 'If this is what we are going to
do, we'll have to cut out this much, hang on to the things that
we like and find other things along the way.' I had a great time
working on the piece. We would talk about something, he would
write at night, and then we'd look at it the next day and make
any changes necessary. Then he was around every day while we
were shooting.

America has always been fascinated by gangsters, no matter
what period or administration. It's part of our need, as a young
country, to create our own mythology. During Roosevelt's time
gangsters were obviously big; under Nixon, which must have
been the time of *The Godfather*, they were big too. I think if you
look over the last ten years, there would be a batch of gangster
movies year in, year out. I don't know when you would consider
them in or out. I think *The Godfather* redefined the gangster
movie because it became a family saga, and gave it a different
slant to what had gone before it. The Bugsy Siegel story had been

60 Bugsy Siegel (Warren Beatty) stands by his creation
in *Bugsy* (1991)

worked on by a number of different people over the years, and I know that there have supposedly been three or four scripts out there about him. I think the fascination stemmed from his being on the one hand a gangster, and on the other the man who invented Las Vegas. But no one could quite fashion a successful script about this incredibly colourful gangster.

I think *Bugsy* works not as a typical gangster movie – there's not a lot of killing or shooting in it – but as a portrait of an obsessive romantic, because of his involvement with Virginia Hill. It really is a love affair, but in an erotic, sick, psychotic way – whatever adjective you want to toss in there would be applicable. I think that's what makes it work, as well as the fact that he invented Las Vegas. And all this is against the period of Hollywood at its peak, during the war years, when the city was at its most glamorous. Bugsy Siegel was accepted by the Hollywood community; he went to all the parties – he was like a movie star who didn't make movies. They say he had the charisma of a movie star, and he even made a private screen test, which is now lost. One of his best friends was George Raft, and we even have them together watching a gangster movie during one of the montage sequences in the film. What Bugsy wanted to do was bring Hollywood and its glamour to the desert. Rather than being a cowboy figure, he desired the elegance of Hollywood, with big entertainers appearing there. Jimmy Durante was to open the Flamingo Hotel, and, of course, Flamingo was the nickname for Virginia Hill.

If someone was to look at *Bugsy* realistically, they would be hard pressed to say that I glamorized him, because we do show a really ugly side to this man. We see him do some truly despicable things. We see his temper, and sometimes his behaviour is very unbecoming, even a joke. But he was glamorized in America because he was attractive, he dressed well, he lived in Beverly Hills – so I expect that kind of criticism. At the same time, although he is often repulsive and repugnant, no one could have got where he did if he hadn't also been charming. Whatever he did in his private life, his public persona was – like, good God, he was a great guy, he was terrific. If he hadn't been like that, he would never have been able to move around town. We

61 Bugsy Siegel (Warren Beatty) at home in Hollywood
in *Bugsy* (1991)

tried to show both sides of his character; and remember that we are talking about a character in a certain period, a very glamorous place and time.

Obviously the movie challenges an audience initially, because although this is an amazingly charismatic character, right at the start of the movie he kills a guy, point blank. We had to show what he was capable of, even though we are saying he will seduce you in the course of the movie. I don't know any other film that begins by doing just that without glossing over or excusing the character's behaviour. What makes him the most dangerous of people is that he blends into society, and is seen to be charming and caring and so on. To me there's an irony in that he does a lot of very uncomfortable things, but the movie has a sophistication and a kind of patina so that we don't immediately recognize how crude and uncomfortable those acts are. And that's what the leading character is all about.

I wanted the look of the film to be related to the period, and how attractive that was. I wanted to avoid the dark browns of *The Godfather*, and of course we were out in California, so it was a totally different look anyway from the sombre tones of the East Coast. On the other hand, I didn't want bright, gaudy colours, but something a little more muted. And I didn't want the kind of glamour that comes from using fog filters, and in fact we didn't use a lot of smoke; we went for a cleaner, simpler approach.

With *Bugsy*, what intrigued me was that I had never done anything termed 'romantic', and I wasn't sure that I could make it work, that I wouldn't fall on my face trying to do it. At the time I had another script I felt very good about, so I was asking myself – Can I do this? Can I pull that off in terms of a certain romanticism? Because we're dealing here with the slightly psychotic behaviour of two people who are all over each other, so there's a dark side to the relationship. And at the same time, could I show a man with an obsessive dream that is incredibly cock-eyed? Can I put those two elements together and make it work? That's what I was curious about. I loved the characters and the great dialogue that Toback had given them. Most movies today don't have very good dialogue. They're more visually driven, with all kinds of acrobatic camerawork. I felt there was a place for a movie with exceptionally good dialogue, with lines that you could remember, so I was taken by that.

It was a nice situation to be with Toback and work and talk things over together. I don't remember what in the world we did to get us where we got to, but we spent a lot of time putting the script into its final shape. Both Toback and Beatty had done a lot of research during all those years they had spent on it, so what I tried to do was pick up on some details and say, 'Hey, what if I was to use this?' You can't be faithful to every date and place and all the events that took place. We collapsed the whole story into a much shorter time frame, because otherwise the film would have spanned ten or fifteen years, and that didn't suit what we wanted to do.

Originally, Warren wanted to do a New York Jewish accent. He tried it, but to me it made the character less interesting because this *Guys and Dolls* way of speaking became a distraction. Now Bugsy was trying to reinvent himself, and disassociate himself from his background. He did work periodically on his elocution to that end. So we opened the film with him practising this phrase, 'Twenty dwarves took turns doing handstands on the carpet', and then I realized during the shooting that we could use it like an internal motor. When certain things happened to him, like having to shoot Harry Greenberg, then the simple repetition of those lines would be coloured by that moment.

I think *Bugsy* is like nothing Warren has ever done before. I think he is much more mature than he has ever been before. I watched *Reds* again and I realized that he could never have done Bugsy Siegel at that time, because he would have been too much of a kid in a way. He didn't have the weight that he has now and I think was necessary to play Bugsy. Of course, Bugsy was forty-two when he was killed and Warren is fifty-three, but when you look at people of that time they all looked older. And seeing Warren in *Reds*, when he was in his early forties, he looked like a guy who was in his thirties. I don't know anyone else who could have pulled off the part, because Bugsy was really attractive, and not some kind of thug.

Warren does need a few more takes to do the work than I was

62 Bugsy Siegel (Warren Beatty) watches his own screen test in
Bugsy (1991)

used to. Actually, I think he can do it in less takes, but he's accustomed to that way of working. I think it's a shame that he did so few movies in the 1980s – *Reds* and *Ishtar* – then *Dick Tracy* in 1990. I'd like to have seen nine movies from him in the 1980s, and then I think we could have seen a real body of work from him, because he's become an underrated actor. He may be even better than he realizes. But because he didn't work a lot, we tend to classify him as a good-looking actor rather than an intelligent one, and I'm sure he could have shown us a lot more.

The name of Annette Bening came up at some point, and I remember meeting her at the Bel Air Hotel. We sat and talked, and I found her intelligent, as well as possessing a good sense of humour. I had seen only a little of her work, but I thought she could say some of these tough lines Virginia has to deliver, and be amusing with them. Some people say tough lines and they just come out tough. Others say them and you're a little amused by it without them being funny. So that seemed correct to me, and Warren liked her a lot and admired her work. So we went from there. Virginia is a tough role, I think potentially one of the outstanding female roles. You know she's real; she's tough and she is vulnerable. She knows what she wants, she stands up to Bugsy and goes toe to toe with him at times. She's both funny and serious, everything that goes to make a great female role.

I believe we had a very competent group of actors. Ben Kingsley might not have been an obvious choice as Meyer Lansky, and when his name came up I said, 'I love Ben Kingsley, but I wonder if he can do an American accent?' I wanted to meet him, but matters between agencies got confusing and it never happened. Then very close to filming he had to come to Los Angeles for some function, so we got to meet and talked and he read the script. I said, 'I have to be honest with you. You're a great actor, there's no question, but if we can't pull off an American accent for this movie, it's not going to work.' This was on a Friday, so he said, 'Give me the weekend and I'll play with a scene, though it'll be like roughing it, because I want to have more time and we've only got a weekend.' He came back to us on Monday, we went over it – and he was there, it was great. What I really appreciated was that he did something a lot of American actors

63 The charming psychopath Bugsy Siegel as portrayed by
Warren Beatty in *Bugsy* (1991)
64 Virginia Hill (Annette Bening) pursued by Bugsy Siegel
(Warren Beatty) in *Bugsy* (1991)

wouldn't do. The three of us – Warren, myself and Ben – sat round and tried it out, because there was this problem. It could have been a stumbling block, yet he had no reservations about it. We said it was fine, we got him his wardrobe, and that was that. And I took a couple of wild shots like that, such as casting Bill Graham[1] as Lucky Luciano, and he was very good too. Harvey Keitel just got hold of the role of Mickey Cohen, intuitively understood it, and all we had to do really was to change him physically.

Certainly *Bugsy* was logistically complex. You constantly were trying to find ways to keep costs down, but movies just keep costing more. Somebody told me the other day that they did a play on Broadway: in 1972 it cost $190,000 and the same play now would cost $6 million! There are so few ways around the problem, even when so much money gets deferred. Even with a lot of Warren's money deferred, and mine too, you still end up with a below-the-line[2] cost in the $20s. But in the final analysis, whether a movie costs $6 million or $60 million, it's the same situation when you are making it. Whatever the cost of the movie, when you are trying to realize every day's work, that part doesn't make any difference to me. And I think that's true for most directors, because you're trying to deliver everything that you can deliver.

With *Bugsy*, it was made basically within the parameters of what we talked about. It was not an extravagant shoot. In the entire movie, I think we eliminated one scene from all of the stuff that we shot. So we were certainly not wasteful in that respect. I was intrigued by several areas, because this is the strongest story piece that I have worked on. Your obligations were to deal with the story – you constantly have to be aware of it – and while going from event to event, it's a matter of, let's colour it, let's give it all the character work that we can. But it's the story that drives the piece, so in the shooting my obligation was not to be too loose, not to drop the ball. You have to be aware of those circumstances.

I'm sure most people watching *Bugsy* wouldn't think of it as being fast-paced. It's a little bit like being on an airplane: if you're going at 300 miles an hour or at some point 3,000 miles an hour, you can't tell the difference. If you watched it scene by scene, it is extremely fast, much faster than normal rhythms. But in the context of a movie that runs two hours and fifteen minutes, it seems perfectly normal. I feel that the dialogue just zips along, but, as I've often said, I think that the dialogue is the action, and there is a drive and a vitality to this particular style.

On Bugsy, *as with all the features Levinson has directed, he worked with his regular film editor, Stu Linder. An Oscar-winner for co-editing* Grand Prix *(1966), Linder had worked with Sam O'Steen and, after spending five years sailing around the world, returned to Hollywood in 1981 and was subsequently chosen by Mark Johnson and Levinson to edit* Diner.

With some directors, the editor does an assembly of the movie, then the director looks at it, and then they work together from there. I don't do any assemblage of the movie. If I'm actually at a studio and shooting when the dailies come in, I don't have a lot of conversations at that stage. I will just watch the dailies with Stu on the editing machine, and as we are running through I'll say, 'I like this take, I like that', and then we will start to assemble a scene from them. Then I'll come in and work with the editor on that scene, and we'll just keep building it and refining it. So when we watch the movie for the very first time from beginning to end, it is far removed from any assemblage. It really has been defined many times along the way. Then we'll obviously keep cutting from that stage on, constantly talking about things, and I may even call the editor about other ideas from the set. That way I never let the movie get particularly far away, and the processes of shooting and editing are going on hand to mouth, in a way.

Although my scripts are tightly written, in the end the interesting thing is to create an atmosphere of freedom and yet ensure that the actors don't stray very far. Sometimes, out of the rigidity of following a script, they think there is something wrong and try to find another way to go about it. I basically say, 'Let's try another direction', because the scene itself may not be the enemy, but I don't want them to feel that is the way it has to be.

65 Barry Levinson directs Warren Beatty in *Bugsy* (1991), with
Baltimore Pictures producer Mark Johnson in attendance

Because if they find something else, it might be fine too, and it allows for the opportunity to sneak up on a scene and test the waters until you can arrive at exactly where you want to be. I will try anything to get where I want to be in a scene.

For the big scene on the sound stage where Virginia Hill meets Bugsy for the first time and says to him, 'Why don't you go outside and jerk yourself a soda?' I said to the production designer Dennis Gassner, 'This conversation has a real spin to it but the setting seems boring.' As I saw it, he wants to be a movie star and she wants to be a movie star, and neither of them ever became that. And here they were at the shooting of *Manpower*,[3] which we were using for the scene. As we were running a tape of the movie, at the end there is a scene on a hill by a gas station, and I put the image on freeze and said, 'Dennis, look at this. Let's take the gas station on the hill, and everybody would be going over it to get to their dressing rooms. She would be going in that direction, Bugsy would stop her, and then we can play the scene on the movie set.' Playing it against that fake world would be like giving them a glamorous surrounding which they're not actually part of. It would give it a little bit of an edge. And this was early on in the discussions. Sometimes you have a set which you know will be there, and you'll find something in the shooting of it that will add to a scene.

Sometimes it's very clear in my head what I want to do, and when I arrive on the set and as I begin to block it, new ideas come to mind. I think, now, if he goes around like that, then we can dolly round behind him and then she will turn and whatever – it just begins to express itself. Sometimes I will stay close to my intentions and the blocking will be exactly what I had in mind. I think you have to take advantage of the moment. An actor may perform an action that tells me a whole new way to shoot a scene. Stylistically, you know in your mind how you are going to handle a movie. But given the mechanics of a scene, you may want to do it in one shot as opposed to cutting it up. For example, when Virginia comes into Bugsy's house for the first time, she says, 'I don't want to interrupt your pantomime', and he replies, 'No, no.' 'What were you watching?' 'Nothing, just a little newsreel.' Then she walks behind the screen and he follows her,

66 George Raft and Marlene Dietrich in Raoul Walsh's
Manpower (1941)
67 Bugsy Siegel (Warren Beatty) and Virginia Hill (Annette Bening)
in the silhouetted embrace in *Bugsy* (1991)

and as she comes out the other side he is silhouetted behind the screen and says, 'Was it too early to put a ring on your finger?' 'Nothing's too early that fits.' Then they go back behind the screen so that they are both silhouetted. And as they move we keep moving with the camera and end up with just their silhouettes. The whole scene is done in one take. And I didn't know that's the way I wanted to do the scene. I only knew I wanted to be behind the screen on the lines, 'Do you always talk this much before you do it?' 'I only talk this much before I'm going to kill someone.' And then they kiss. I didn't know how I was going to handle what went before. I knew there was a projector and a light, and I thought of having them walk through the projector light. When we began to block it, it just evolved into one take from coming through the door to the kiss. It took a while to evolve, because I never want to force the blocking. I might do fake moves to accomplish a particular shot, but it's just so that I can organically arrive at a combination of an idea and what else might evolve from the scene.

Bugsy *was nominated for ten Academy Awards, but in the event it won only two, for Best Art Direction (Dennis Gassner) and Best Costume Design (Albert Wolsky). However, it was voted Best Picture at the Golden Globe Awards and by the Los Angeles Film Critics' Association, who also voted Levinson Best Director. Although Beatty's film had been passed on by Disney, who felt it was too expensive,* Bugsy *was to prove considerably more successful than that studio's other costly gangster project,* Billy Bathgate.

   Bugsy *was a collaboration between Warren Beatty's production company and Barry Levinson's Baltimore Pictures, which, since* Avalon, *had been looking to cast its net wider than Levinson's own films.*

We started Baltimore Pictures mainly to come up with work I wouldn't necessarily direct, but that I felt would be valid to get made. Mark and I tried to develop some material and some writers and put together a company that had some vitality to it, making films that were a slight departure from the mainstream product. If I wasn't interested in specific work done by certain writers, then perhaps someone else might be. Already there has been Steven Soderbergh's *Kafka*, and there is a script called *Wilder Napalm*, which will hopefully be shot in October or November of 1992. The intention is that I wouldn't interfere with choices and decisions made by the directors in question, but that they go their own way. At best you could say these projects are very much left of centre. At the same time, through the production company I am developing projects for myself, including an adaptation of the novel *Brotherly Love* by its author, Pete Dexter, who wrote *Paris Trout*.

Brotherly Love details three decades of a Philadelphia Irish family at loggerheads with the Mafia, and promises considerably less glamour in its portrayal of mob violence than Bugsy. *But while that film was still in development, in late February 1992 Levinson began shooting* Toys, *the original script he and Valerie Curtin penned that was to have been his directorial début. The story concerns a maniacal general forced into early retirement who, after the death of his brother, takes over the family toy company and begins developing toys that have full military capacity. War then breaks out when his nephew and niece, who would seem to be the rightful heirs, try to stop their irresponsible uncle.*

After its rejection by 20th Century Fox, Columbia had tried to set Toys *up to follow* Good Morning, Vietnam, *only for the project to disappear along with outgoing studio boss David Puttnam. But with a new studio chief at Fox, Leonard Goldberg, the film was rescheduled for shooting in England, with a budget that had gone from $6 million to $20 million. The weak dollar in the late 1980s kept costs soaring, and Levinson himself decided to postpone the project.*

We originally sold *Toys* to Fox back in 1978, and it was going to be my first film as a director. But then Sherry Lansing joined the studio and she didn't think it was funny, and others agreed. You couldn't mention a movie that would conjure up the image of this film, so for the executives there was an absence of an idea of what it might be. That made it rather dangerous. I think now that even if they can't see the type of movie it will be, enough is known about my work for them to trust me and know that I'm not totally insane in wanting to make it. They can be assured that I will accomplish something without it being a threat.

The script has evolved over the years. The basic idea still applies, because I think the world has come closer to the General's idea that the cost of weaponry is too high, and through the manufacture of toys there's a way of making smaller weaponry which is cheaper. It's the difference between paying $1 million for one plane or building a million toy planes. Because the economy cannot support the militaries of the world, this is the future for them. With computerization and high technology, it becomes like a video arcade game – and, of course, children can fly the planes!

I think the design element of the film was always going to be extreme, but over the years I've changed my ideas to keep it fresh and always different from what's been seen before. And I've pushed the design element further and further, so the movie has become stranger and stranger as time goes on. Nando[4] has a great background in everything from opera to film, and I felt he had a very good sensibility for what was required, which was a surreal, Magritte-like look. Our reference point was the toy-makers of the 1800s, a kind of magic workshop. These places don't necessarily exist any more, so what we're trying to do is create a magical workshop of the 1990s that is big business in America.

A number of years ago I thought of John Cleese for the General, but we could never work it out. I really liked the idea of an American being trapped in an English body. Then Michael Gambon's name came up, and we got a chance to meet. I want all the characters to be off-centre. Robin Williams was cast some time ago as Leslie, and he made perfect sense. Joan Cusack came to us for a meeting quite by chance, and I just thought she would be terrific for Alsatia. And L. L. Cool J, the black rapper, plays Michael Gambon's son, who of course is Robin's cousin. The fact that he should have a black cousin somehow made perfect sense to me, because it's never an issue in the film.

The original draft back in 1979 had the idea of virtual reality

68 Levinson directs Michael Gambon as the mad General Leland
Presswell in *Toys* (1992)

69 Levinson directs Robin Williams and Joan Cusack as Leslie and
Alsatia in *Toys* (1992)

before the fad came to be. As a result, I have now backed off that a little. We certainly play upon the aspects of military computer games that children have now. There is a certain degree of tasteful revenge on the whole arcade-game mentality that has taken over a lot of movies today. It's the first time for me to do an out and out comedy since I left television, and though there are political ideas inherent in the script, I don't wish to belabour the issue. I have always been mystified by people seeing it as a dark film, a black comedy. This is much warmer, with the characters strongly relating to one another. And, of course, it's about a family.

Notes

1 Bill Graham, who was killed in a helicopter crash after completing his role in *Bugsy*, was the famous rock impresario who produced concerts at San Francisco's Fillmore, as well as managing tours for Bob Dylan, The Rolling Stones and many others. His previous film appearance was in *Apocalypse Now* (1979).

2 Below-the-line costs are usually fixed production overheads, excluding the fees, expenses and salaries for the stars, writer, producer and director.

3 *Manpower*, directed by Raoul Walsh in 1941, was a Warner Brothers production that brought together Edward G. Robinson and George Raft as two power linemen in competition for the love of a café hostess, played by Marlene Dietrich.

4 Ferdinando Scarfiotti has designed for the stage, opera and cinema, and is best known for his collaboration with director Bernardo Bertolucci and cinematographer Vittorio Storaro on *The Conformist* (1969) and *The Last Emperor* (1987). In the USA, he has worked with Paul Schrader on *American Gigolo* (1980) and Brian De Palma on *Scarface* (1983).

70 Barry Levinson (1990)

Filmography

Special note: Barry Levinson (the subject of this book) should not be mistaken for another Barry Levinson (1932–87), for their filmographies have sometimes been confusingly elided. The 'other' Barry Levinson was born in New York and lived in Britain for many years. He formed the theatrical agency of Savan-Levinson-Parker and a number of film companies, and worked as a film and television producer and occasional writer. His film credits include First Love *(1970),* The Night Visitor *(1970),* The Amazing Mr Blunden *(1972),* The Internecine Project *(1974) and* Who? *(1974). His television credits include* Catholics *(1973),* Displaced Persons *(1985) and* Suspicion *(1988).*

Television

1969

The Lohman and Barkley Show

Featuring: Al Lohman, Roger Barkley
Writers/performers: Barry Levinson, Craig Nelson and others
Station: KNBC-TV
90 mins

1970

The Tim Conway Comedy Hour
Variety show mainly with sketch comedy, hosted by comedian Tim Conway, which ran three months.

Featuring: Tim Conway, McLean Stevenson, Art Metrano, The Tom Hansen Dancers, Sally Struthers, Bonnie Boland, Belland and Somerville and guests
Producers: Bill Hobin, Ron Clark, Sam Bobrick

Writers: Barry Levinson, Craig Nelson, Rudy De Luca
Network: CBS
60 mins

1972

The Marty Feldman Comedy Machine

Comedy variety show with mainly visual sketches featuring the bug-eyed comedian.

Featuring: Marty Feldman, Spike Milligan, Bob Todd, Hugh Paddick
Guests included: Orson Welles, Groucho Marx, Barbara Feldon, Art Carney, Roger Moore, Marsha Hunt, Randy Newman
Producers: Larry Gelbart, Colin Clews
Writers: Barry Levinson, John Antrobus, Rudy De Luca, Chris Allen, Pat McCormick
Production company: ATV
Network: ITV (Britain)/ABC (USA)
14 x 60 mins (30 mins in USA)

The John Byner Comedy Hour

Summer variety series in which the majority of comedy sketches used Byner's ability as an impressionist in movie spoofs, including *The Godfather* and, interestingly, George C. Scott's *Patton* as the president of a toy factory.

Featuring: John Byner, Patty Deutsch, R. G. Brown, Linda Sublette, Gary Miller, Dennis Flannigan, The Ray Charles Orchestra and guests
Executive producers: Nick Sevano, Rich Eutis, Al Rogers
Writers: Barry Levinson, Craig Nelson, Rudy De Luca
Network: CBS
60 mins

1973

Comedy News

Featuring: Andrew Duncan, Kenneth Mars, Fannie Flagg, Marian Mercer, Anthony Holland, Richard Pryor, Mort Sahl, Stan Freberg, Bob & Ray
Executive producer: Sylvester (Pat) Weaver
Writers: Mort Sahl, Barry Levinson and others
Network: ABC
90 mins

'*It was a late-night show which parodied the news, following the tradition of the British programme* That Was the Week That Was.' *(BL)*

1974-5

The Carol Burnett Show

Highly popular and successful comedy variety show that ran for eleven years until 1978 (ten editions were shown on BBC2 in 1970). The show would normally consist of sketches spoofing other TV series and feature films, stand-up routines and musical numbers, as well as Burnett and the guest star answering questions from the studio audience. Two recurring sketches cast Burnett and Korman as an aged couple and as an uptight married couple, Ed and Eunice. The show was revived in November 1991.

Featuring: Carol Burnett, Harvey Korman, Lyle Waggoner, Vicki Lawrence, Tim Conway, The Earnest Flatt Dancers, The Peter Matz Orchestra and guests
Executive producer: Joe Hamilton
Writers: Barry Levinson, Ed Simmons, Gary Belkin, Roger Beatty, Arnie Kogen, Bill Richmond, Gene Perret, Rudy De Luca, Dick Clair, Jenna McMahon, Barry Harmon
Network: CBS
60 mins

1975

Hot L Baltimore

Situation comedy based on the award-winning Broadway play by Lanford Wilson of the same title, set in the lobby of the run-down Hotel Baltimore, the sign of which had lost the 'e'. Considered controversial at the time for its racy dialogue and sexual innuendo, the show ran for four months.

Cast: James Cromwell (*Bill Lewis*), Richard Masur (*Clifford Ainsley*), Conchata Ferrell (*April Green*), Al Freeman Jr (*Charles Bingham*), Jeannie Linero (*Suzy Marta Rocket*), Gloria Le Roy (*Millie*), Robin Wilson (*Jackie*), Stan Gottlieb (*Mr Morse*), Lee Bergere (*George*), Henry Calvert (*Gordon*), Charlotte Rae (*Mrs Bellotti*)
Producers: Ron Clark, Gene Marcione
Executive producer: Rod Parker
Writers: Barry Levinson, Ron Clark, Rod Parker
Network: ABC
30 mins

1976

The Rich Little Show

Comedy variety series that ran for six months, featuring impressionist Rich Little as host, with a regular monologue and a number of sketches.

Featuring: Rich Little, Charlotte Rae, Julie McWhirter, R. G. Brown, Mel Bishop, Joe Baker and guests

Producers: Rich Eustis, Al Rogers
Executive producer: Jerry Goldstein
Writers: Barry Levinson, Ron Clark, Rudy De Luca, Ray Jessel, Jim Mulligan
Network: NBC
60 mins

1978

Peeping Times
Featuring: Alan Oppenheimer, David Letterman, Richard Libertini, Ron Carey, David Hall, Valerie Curtin, Johnie Dexter
Producers: Barry Levinson, Rudy De Luca
Executive producers: David Frost, Marvin Minoff
Writers: Barry Levinson, Rudy De Luca, Bill Richmond, Gene Perret, Robert Illes, James Stein, Christopher Guest
Network: NBC
60 mins

'It was a parody of the 60 Minutes investigative-reporting-style programme. We only did a pilot. The network thought it was too strange. The irony is that we had two anchor people, and NBC said that one of the guys didn't test very well and that I should get rid of him. I said, "No, he's very, very funny", and refused to change him. And that was David Letterman.' (BL)

1983

Diner
Pilot for a series (never made) based on the characters from the film. In the diner, Modell boasts that the guys would be perfectly cool if a famous star like Jane Russell was to walk in – they'd just offer her a cup of coffee and ask her to sit down for a chat. Eddie returns from his honeymoon, claiming he isn't going to hang out at the diner any more. But old habits die hard.

Cast: Paul Reiser (*Modell*), Michael Binder (*Eddie*), Michael Madsen (*Boogie*), James Spader (*Fenwick*), Max Cantor (*Shrevie*), Mandy Kaplan (*Beth*), Alison LaPlaca (*Elise*), Jessica James, Robert Pastorelli, Amie Mazer, Ted Bafaloukas
Producer: Mark Johnson
Executive producers: Barry Levinson, Jerry Weintraub
Director: Barry Levinson
Writer: Barry Levinson
Network: CBS
30 mins

71 David Letterman, Rudy De Luca and Barry Levinson discuss
their script in *Peeping Times* (1978)

Stopwatch: Thirty Minutes of Investigative Ticking

Another satire on the *60 Minutes*-style programme, including reports on a blind man teaching seeing-eye dogs, a boxing nun, criminals serving time by doing chores for the households they burgled, and Murray Resnick, a US government agent, collecting debts from foreign countries.

Cast: Michael G. Kelly (*Ron Ramsgate, host*), Alan Oppenheimer (*Chris Mantock, host*), Bill Kirchenbauer (*Angry Arnie, consumer reporter*)
Executive producers: Barry Levinson, Rudy De Luca, Peter Locke
Director: Rudy De Luca
Writers: Barry Levinson, Rudy De Luca, J. J. Barry, George Gipe
Network: HBO
30 mins

'*This was similar to the format we tried for* Peeping Times, *but it was still considered too unusual, too nuts. We figured there was no actual need to go out to the places where we were supposed to be reporting, that was a waste of time and money. So if we were meant to be in New Jersey, we'd say, 'We're standing in the foothills of the New Jersey mountain range', though we weren't disguising the fact it was actually the San Fernando Valley. Or if we were supposed to be outside the FBI building, rather than go there, we'd just have a guy standing by a brick wall and put up a sign saying "FBI Building". Some of our sketches were considered too distasteful, like a commercial to try and get guys to join the church and become priests, with music numbers and even a couple of priests break-dancing. I haven't seen the show in a long time, so it may not be funny any more, but at the time I enjoyed it.*' (BL)

1984

The Investigators

A similar venture to *Stopwatch*, featuring the 'Crusading reporters of the air' in a satire on investigative journalism.

Cast: Charles Rocket (*Truman Kruman, reporter*), Bill Kirchenbauer (*Angry Arnie, consumer reporter*)
Executive producers: Barry Levinson, Rudy De Luca, Peter Locke
Director: Barry Levinson
Writers: Barry Levinson, Rudy De Luca, George Gipe, Jurgen Wolff
Network: HBO
25 mins

1987

Harry

Situation comedy in which Arkin played a wheeler-dealer head of purchasing at a city hospital.

Cast: Alan Arkin (*Harry Porschak*), Holland Taylor (*Nurse Sandy Clifton*), Thom Bray (*Lawrence Pendleton*), Matt Craven (*Bobby Kratz*), Barbara Dana (*Dr Sandy Clifton*), Kurt Knudson (*Wyatt Lockhart*), Richard Lewis (*Richard Breskin*)
Producers: Don Van Atta, Shelley Zellman
Executive producers: Barry Levinson, Mark Johnson, Alan Arkin
Supervising producer-writer: Gary Jacobs
Network: ABC
6 x 30 mins

1990

Time-Warner Presents the Earth Day Special

Taped live on 22 April 1990, a TV special in which prominent celebrities from film, television, sports and music publicized the global crisis of pollution, starvation and the resources shortage.

Production company: Warner Bros Inc./People of the Earth Entertainment/Sum Entertainment
Co-writer: Barry Levinson
120 mins

'I wrote a sketch with Robin Williams and Dustin Hoffman for them to play, and I was there for the shooting. It was just one segment in the piece, and I think it dealt with a lawyer talking to someone else about everything from the ozone layer to the destruction of our water.' (BL)

Cinema

As producer

1991

Kafka

Prague, 1919. Kafka, a clerk in an insurance company, becomes both suspect and amateur detective when a colleague is found murdered.

Production company: Baltimore Pictures/Renn/Pricel SA
Producers: Stuart Cornfield, Harry Benn
Executive producers: Paul Rassam, Mark Johnson
Director: Steven Soderbergh
Screenplay: Lem Dobbs
Photography (b/w & colour): Walt Loyd
Production design: Gavin Bocquet, Tony Woollard
Music: Cliff Martinez

Cast: Jeremy Irons (*Kafka*), Theresa Russell (*Gabriela*), Joel Grey (*Burgel*), Ian Holm (*Dr Murnau*), Jeroen Krabbe (*Bizzlebeck*), Armin Mueller-Stahl (*Grubach*), Alec Guinness (*The Chief Clerk*), Brian Glover (*Castle Henchman*)
98 mins

1992

Wilder Napalm
Two brothers with pyrotechnical powers become involved in a romantic triangle.

Production company: Baltimore Pictures
Producers: Mark Johnson, Stuart Cornfield
Executive producer: Barrie Osbourne
Director: Glenn Gordon Caron
Screenplay: Vince Gilligan
Photography: Jerry Hartleben
Cast: Debra Winger, Dennis Quaid, Arliss Howard, Jim Varney, M. Emmet Walsh

As actor

1976

Silent Movie
Director: Mel Brooks
as *Executive*

1977

High Anxiety
Director: Mel Brooks
as *Bellboy*

1981

History of the World – Part 1
Director: Mel Brooks
as *Column Salesman*

1988

Rain Man
Director: Barry Levinson
as *Doctor*

As writer

1974

Street Girls
Irv, the owner of a topless club in Eugene, Oregon, tries to persuade one of
his dancers, Angel, to turn to prostitution. He turns for aid to Mario, Angel's
drug-dealing lover, who hooks her on heroin. Angel's father, Sven, searches for
his daughter with the help of another dancer, Sally. Irv retaliates by murdering
Sally and having Sven beaten up, but Angel is finally rescued by her father.

Production company: BMP Productions
Producers: Paul Pompian, Jeff Begun
Director: Michael Miller
Screenplay: Michael Miller, Barry Levinson
Photography: Bob Wilson
Music: Terry Smith
Cast: Carl Case (*Sally*), Paul Pompian (*Irv*), Art Burke (*Sven*), Chris Souder
(*Angel*), Jay Derringer (*Mario*)
84 mins

'*A friend of mine was making it, and asked me if I'd come up and help him write
some scenes. It was a pretty crazy affair, and I ended up assisting on camera
too.*' (BL)

1976

Silent Movie
Famous director Mel Funn plans to make a comeback from alcoholic oblivion
and, with the aid of friends Marty Eggs and Dom Bell, he approaches the bank-
rupt Big Picture Studios with the proposal to make a silent movie. They set
about enticing a number of Hollywood stars to join their cast. The giant corpo-
ration Engulf and Devour, eager to take over the studio, try to stop Funn's successful plan by stealing the film and using a seductive spy, Vilma Kaplan, to put
the director back on the bottle. Minutes before the crucial sneak preview, Funn
is restored to sobriety and the film is found. The audience response is ecstatic.

Production company: Crossbow Productions
Producer: Michael Hertzberg

Director: Mel Brooks
Screenplay: Mel Brooks, Ron Clark, Rudy De Luca, Barry Levinson
Photography: Paul Lohmann
Editors: John C. Howard, Stanford C. Allen
Production designer: Al Brenner
Music: John Morris
Cast: Mel Brooks (*Mel Funn*), Marty Feldman (*Marty Eggs*), Dom DeLuise (*Dom Bell*), Bernadette Peters (*Vilma Kaplan*), Sid Caesar (*Studio Chief*), Harold Gould (*Engulf*), Ron Carey (*Devour*), Carol Arthur (*Pregnant Lady*), Liam Dunn (*Newsvendor*), Fritz Field (*Maître d'*), Chuck McCann (*Studio Gate Guard*), Valerie Curtin (*Intensive Care Nurse*), Yvonne Wilder (*Studio Chief's Secretary*), Arnold Soboloff (*Acupuncture Man*), Patrick Campbell (*Motel Bellhop*), Harry Ritz (*Man in Tailor Shop*), Charlie Callas (*Blind Man*), Henny Youngman (*Fly-in-Soup Man*), Eddie Ryder (*British Officer*), Robert Lussier (*Projectionist*), Al Hopson, Rudy De Luca, Barry Levinson, Howard Hesserman, Lee Delano and Jack Riley (*Executives*), Inga Neisen, Sivi Aberg and Erica Hagen (*Beautiful Blondes*), Burt Reynolds, James Caan, Liza Minnelli, Anne Bancroft, Marcel Marceau and Paul Newman (*Themselves*)
87 mins

1977

High Anxiety

Dr Richard H. Thorndyke is appointed to be the new head of the Psycho-Neurotic Institute for the Very, Very Nervous, but the assistant director, Dr Charles Montague, and head nurse, Charlotte Diesel, plot to remove him. Thorndyke encounters Victoria Brisbane, who has lost touch with her wealthy father since he was admitted to the clinic, and they team up with the doctor's old mentor, Professor Lilloman, who counsels Thorndyke on his neurosis about heights. Together they expose the conspirators and Thorndyke is cured of his 'high anxiety'.

Production company: Crossbow Productions
Producer: Mel Brooks
Director: Mel Brooks
Screenplay: Mel Brooks, Rudy De Luca, Ron Clark, Barry Levinson
Photography: Paul Lohmann
Editor: John C. Howard
Production designer: Peter Wooley
Music: John Morris
Cast: Mel Brooks (*Richard H. Thorndyke*), Madeline Kahn (*Victoria Brisbane*), Cloris Leachman (*Nurse Charlotte Diesel*), Harvey Korman (*Dr Charles Montague*), Ron Carey (*Brophy*), Howard Morris (*Professor Lilloman*), Dick Van Patten (*Dr Philip Wentworth*), Jack Riley (*Desk Clerk*), Charlie Callas (*Cocker Spaniel*), Ron Clark (*Zachary Cartwright*), Rudy De Luca (*Killer*), Barry Levinson (*Bellboy*), Lee Delano (*Norton*), Richard Stahl (*Dr Baxter*), Darrell Zwerling (*Dr Eckhardt*), Murphy Dunne (*Piano Player*), Al Hopson

(*Man Who Is Shot*), Bob Ridgely (*Flasher*), Albert J. Whitlock (*Arthur Brisbane*)
94 mins

1979

. . . And Justice for All

Angry young Baltimore lawyer Arthur Kirkland is bailed out of jail for a contempt charge by a client involved in a traffic accident. One of Arthur's enemies is Judge Fleming, who, because of a missed deadline, refuses to admit new evidence in court that would exonerate one of Arthur's clients, Jeff McCallaugh. Under scrutiny by the Ethics Committee, with one of whose members, Gail Packer, he is having an affair, Arthur is coerced into defending Fleming on a rape charge. Meanwhile, Arthur has promised to defend a black transvestite, Ralph Agee, but when the case has to be taken on by an incompetent colleague, Agee is sent back to jail, where he hangs himself. Fleming refuses to help Arthur in securing a release for McCallaugh, who finally goes berserk and is shot. The traffic-accident client shows Arthur some compromising photographs of Fleming, who admits to his misconduct without remorse. Still obliged to defend Fleming, Arthur finally breaks down in court, makes a public protest, and is escorted out.

Production company: Malton Films, for Columbia
Producers: Norman Jewison, Patrick Palmer
Director: Norman Jewison
Screenplay: Valerie Curtin, Barry Levinson
Photography: Victor J. Kemper
Editor: John F. Burnett
Production designer: Richard MacDonald
Music: Dave Grusin
Cast: Al Pacino (*Arthur Kirkland*), Jack Warden (*Judge Rayford*), John Forsythe (*Judge Fleming*), Lee Strasberg (*Grandpa Sam*), Jeffrey Tambor (*Jay Porter*), Christine Lahti (*Gail Packer*), Sam Levene (*Arnie*), Robert Christian (*Ralph Agee*), Thomas Waites (*Jeff McCallaugh*), Larry Bryggman (*Warren Fresnell*), Craig T. Nelson (*Frank Bowers*), Dominic Chianese (*Carl Travers*), Victor Arnold (*Leo Fauci*), Vincent Beck (*Officer Leary*), Michael Gorrin (*Elderly Man*), Baxter Harris (*Larry*), Joe Morton (*Prison Doctor*)
119 mins

1980

Inside Moves

With a crippled leg after a failed suicide attempt, Roary joins the regulars at Max's bar – 'Wings', who has hooks for hands, the blind 'Stinky', and the wheelchair-bound 'Blue' Lewis – and befriends lame barman Jerry. Roary's inheritance keeps the bar going when the penniless Max suffers a heart attack.

Jerry's former girlfriend, heroin-addict Ann, returns to him, but is reclaimed by her violent pimp, Lucius Porter. Roary persuades a basketball star to loan some money for Jerry to have an operation, which puts him back in the game. Jerry drifts away from his friends, but on his return begins an affair with the bar waitress, Louise, who Roary has fallen in love with. Roary's anger at this prompts Jerry to apologize to his old friends, and Louise becomes Roary's lover. Just before Jerry's first professional game, Ann reappears to shame him, and Roary takes his revenge by making a fool of Lucius Porter.

Production company: Lija Productions for Universal
Producer: Hank Moonjean
Director: Richard Donner
Screenplay: Valerie Curtin, Barry Levinson; based on the novel by Todd Walton
Photography: Laszlo Kovacs
Editor: Frank Morriss
Production designer: Charles Rosen
Music: John Barry
Cast: Jon Savage (*Roary*), David Morse (*Jerry Maxwell*), Diana Scarwid (*Louise*), Amy Wright (*Ann*), Tony Burton (*Lucius Porter*), Bill Henderson (*'Blue' Lewis*), Steve Kahan (*Burt*), Jack O'Leary (*Max Willatowski*), Bert Ramsen (*'Stinky'*), Harold Russell (*'Wings'*), Pepe Serna (*Herrada*), Harold Sylvester (*Alvin Martin*), Arnold Williams (*Benny*), George Brenlin (*Gil*)
113 mins

1982

Best Friends

After years of living together, successful Hollywood screenwriters Richard Babson and Paula McCullen decide secretly to marry. As a honeymoon trip, they travel to their parental homes in the East. In Buffalo, Paula's parents behave very eccentrically and complain about their own married life. In Virginia, Richard's domineering mother insists on a big wedding party, and the strain finally ruptures the relationship. Back in Hollywood the couple are obliged to complete a screenplay together even though they are not on speaking terms. Locked in an office together, they complete the new scenes and repair their marriage.

Production company: Warner Brothers
Producers: Norman Jewison, Patrick Palmer
Director: Norman Jewison
Screenplay: Valerie Curtin, Barry Levinson
Photography: Jordan Cronenworth
Editor: Don Zimmerman
Production designer: Henry Alberti
Music: Michel Legrand
Cast: Burt Reynolds (*Richard Babson*), Goldie Hawn (*Paula McCullen*), Jes-

sica Tandy (*Eleanor McCullen*), Barnard Hughes (*Tim McCullen*), Audra
Lindley (*Ann Babson*), Keenan Wynn (*Tom Babson*), Ron Silver (*Larry Weis-
man*), Carol Locatell (*Nellie Ballou*), Richard Libertini (*Jorge Medina*), Peggy
Walton-Walker (*Carol Brandon*), Noah Hathaway (*Lyle Ballou*), Mikey Martin (*Robbie Ballou*), Helen Page Camp (*Maid*), Joan Pringle (*Doria*)
109 mins

1983

Unfaithfully Yours

Famous conductor Claude Eastman returns to New York after a world tour
and becomes suspicious that his beautiful young wife, Daniella, has been having an affair with solo violinist Max Stein. Although he is mistaken and fails
to find them in a compromising situation, Claude plots to disguise himself as
Max and murder Daniella in sight of the apartment's security cameras, while
creating an audio tape that would incriminate Max. But everything goes disas-
trously wrong, Daniella discovers what Claude has been up to, and the couple
are finally reconciled after rowing in the street.

Production company: 20th Century Fox
Producers: Marvin Worth, Joe Wizan
Director: Howard Zieff
Screenplay: Valerie Curtin, Barry Levinson, Robert Klane; based on the script
for *Unfaithfully Yours* (1948) by Preston Sturges
Photography: David M. Walsh
Editor: Sheldon Kahn
Production designer: Albert Brenner
Music: Bill Conti
Cast: Dudley Moore (*Claude Eastman*), Nastassja Kinski (*Daniella Eastman*),
Armand Assante (*Maximillian Stein*), Albert Brooks (*Norman Robbins*), Cas-
sie Yates (*Carla Robbins*), Richard Libertini (*Giuseppe*), Richard B. Shull (*Jess
Keller*), Jan Triska (*Jerzy Czyrek*), Jane Hallaren (*Janet*), Bernard Behrens (*Bill
Lawrence*), Leonard Mann (*Screen Lover*), Estelle Omens (*Celia*)
96 mins

As director

1982

Diner

Baltimore, 1959. Billy Howard returns home from college to find his old friends
still hanging out at the diner. Shrevie Schreiber, a TV salesman, has married
Beth, but finds they have little to talk about. Eddie Simmons, about to marry
Elise, decides she must pass a football quiz first. Timothy Fenwick has deserted
his wealthy family and taken to drinking. Boogie Sheftell, who works in a

hairdressing salon by day and attends law classes by night to impress girls, has a serious gambling debt of $2,000. Billy offers to marry Barbara, whom he has made pregnant, but finds her more absorbed in her television career. Elise just fails the test, and Eddie calls the wedding off. Boogie is tempted to seduce a depressed Beth and use the occasion as a way of winning a bet, but at the last moment he confesses his plan to her and restores her self-respect. His debt is paid off by Bagel, a friend of his mother, and he agrees to work for him in the home-improvement business. Eddie changes his mind, and the wedding goes ahead. Shrevie and Beth plan a holiday, Fenwick decides to go to Europe, Boogie has become attracted to Jane Chisholm, a wealthy girl who likes to ride horses, and Bill will return to New York to finish his degree.

Production company: MGM/SLM Entertainment
Producer: Jerry Weintraub
Executive producer: Mark Johnson
Director: Barry Levinson
Screenplay: Barry Levinson
Photography: Peter Sova
Editor: Stu Linder
Visual consultant: Gene Rudolf
Music: Bruce Brody, Ivan Kral
Cast: Steve Guttenberg (*Edward 'Eddie' Simmons*), Daniel Stern (*Laurence 'Shrevie' Schreiber*), Mickey Rourke (*Robert 'Boogie' Sheftell*), Kevin Bacon (*Timothy Fenwick Jnr*), Timothy Daly (*William 'Billy' Howard*), Ellen Barkin (*Beth*), Paul Reiser (*Modell*), Kathryn Dowling (*Barbara*), Michael Tucker (*Bagel*), Jessica James (*Mrs Simmons*), Colette Blonigan (*Carol Heathrow*), Kelle Kipp (*Diane*), John Aquino (*Tank*), Richard Pierson (*David Frazer*), Claudia Cron (*Jane Chisholm*), Tait Ruppert (*Methan*), Tom V. V. Tammi (*Howard*), Pam Gail (*1st Stripper*), Lauren Zaganas (*2nd Stripper*), Sharon Zinman (*Elise*), Mark Margolis (*Earl Maget*), Ralph Tabakin (*TV Customer*), Frank Stoegerer (*TV Director*), Nat Benchley (*Technical Director*), Frank Hennessy (*Audio Man*), Marvin Hunter (*Newscaster*), Steve Smith (*Announcer*), Lee Case (*Billy's Father*), Clement Fowler (*Eddie's Father*), Howard 'Chip' Silverman (*Clothing Hustler*)
110 mins

1984

The Natural

The night his father dies, lightning splits a tree on the family farm and from its heart the young Roy Hobbs cuts a baseball bat which he brands 'Wonderboy'. Some years later, after abandoning his sweetheart, Iris, Roy leaves for a professional tryout with the Chicago Cubs. On the way he is challenged by The Whammer, an arrogant baseball star, and wins, much to the amazement of sportswriter Max Mercy. But before his tryout Roy is lured to the apartment of the seductive Harriet Bird, who shoots him. Some years on, Roy announces to Pop Fisher, manager of the New York Knights, that although his past remains a mystery, he has been contracted by Pop's unwanted new partner, the Judge. Although the suspicious Pop holds him back at first, eventually Roy and his 'Wonderboy' prove so successful that the Knights climb up the league. Max Mercy investigates Roy's past, and news of Roy reaches Iris. With the encouragement of the Judge, Pop's beautiful niece Memo begins an affair with Roy, which has a bad effect on his game. One day Iris turns up and reveals to Roy, that, though unmarried, she has a son. Roy's game now improves, and when the Judge tries to bribe him to throw the game that will win the Knights the pennant, he angrily refuses. Memo tries to poison him, and an emergency operation reveals a silver bullet left from an earlier wound. Despite warnings that it may kill him, and using a bat carved by a young fan when 'Wonderboy' breaks, Roy plays his last winning game in the knowledge that the young boy with Iris is his son.

Production company: Tri-Star–Delphi II Productions
Producer: Mark Johnson
Director: Barry Levinson
Screenplay: Roger Towne, Phil Dusenberry; based on the novel by Bernard Malamud
Photography: Caleb Deschanel
Editor: Stu Linder
Production designers: Angelo Graham, Mel Bourne
Music: Randy Newman
Cast: Robert Redford (*Roy Hobbs*), Robert Duvall (*Max Mercy*), Glenn Close (*Iris*), Kim Basinger (*Memo Paris*), Wilford Brimley (*Pop Fisher*), Barbara Hershey (*Harriet Bird*), Robert Prosky (*The Judge*), Richard Farnsworth (*Red Blow*), Joe Don Baker (*The Whammer*), John Finnegan (*Sam Simpson*), Alan Fudge (*Ed Hobbs*), Paul Sullivan Jnr (*Young Roy*), Rachel Hall (*Young Iris*), Robert Rich III (*Ted Hobbs*); the New York Knights: Michael Madsen (*Bump Bailey*), Jon Van Ness (*John Olsen*), Mickey Treanor (*Doc Dizzy*), George Wilkosz (*Bobby Savoy*), Anthony J. Ferrara (*Coach Wilson*), Philip Mankowski (*Hank Benz*), Danny Aiello III (*Emil Lajong*), Joe Castellano (*Allie Stubbs*), Eddie Cipot (*Gabby Laslow*), Ken Grassano (*Al Fowler*), Robert Kalaf (*Cal Baker*), Barry Kivel (*Pat McGee*), Steven Kronovet (*Tommy Hinkle*), James Meyer (*Dutch Schultz*), Michael Starr (*Boone*), Sam Green (*Murphy*)
137 mins (122 mins, British release version)

1985

Young Sherlock Holmes
(British release title *Young Sherlock Holmes and the Pyramid of Fear*)
London, 1870. John Watson joins his new school and meets the young Sherlock Holmes, who is in love with Elizabeth, the daughter of eccentric inventor Professor Waxflatter, whose latest experiment is a flying machine. Holmes is framed by a jealous rival for cheating in exams and is expelled, but takes secret

refuge with Elizabeth. A succession of mysterious deaths caused by frightening hallucinations occur; Professor Waxflatter himself is one of the victims. Watson finds a blow-pipe dropped by a fleeing cloaked figure, and a piece of cloth from the assassin's cloak leads them to a large warehouse in Wapping, where a vast wooden pyramid houses an assembly of cult worshippers. Back at the school they find a photo of a fencing team comprising the three dead men and a mysterious friend of the Professor, Chester Cragwitch. Holmes's former fencing master, Rathe, discovers that Holmes has been staying with Elizabeth, but the trio escape and visit Cragwitch, who tells them of a group of old college boys whose attempts to built a hotel in Egypt resulted in the desecration of a sacred burial ground. A young boy of Anglo-Egyptian descent had sworn revenge then and was now exacting it. Cragwitch is killed by a poison dart, and on their return to the school Holmes and Watson find that Rathe is the avenger. They escape in the Professor's flying machine and rescue Elizabeth, who is about to be sacrificed in the pyramid. After fighting a duel with Holmes, Rathe falls through the ice covering the river. Elizabeth, though, dies in Holmes's arms. As Holmes bids farewell to Watson and the school, elsewhere Rathe signs in at a hotel under the name of Moriarty.

Production company: Amblin Entertainment for Paramount
Producer: Mark Johnson
Director: Barry Levinson
Screenplay: Christopher Columbus
Photography: Stephen Goldblatt
Editor: Stu Linder
Production designer: Norman Reynolds
Music: Bruce Broughton
Cast: Nicholas Rowe (*Sherlock Holmes*), Alan Cox (*John Watson*), Sophie Ward (*Elizabeth*), Anthony Higgins (*Rathe*), Susan Fleetwood (*Mrs Dribb*), Freddie Jones (*Chester Cragwitch*), Nigel Stock (*Waxflatter*), Roger Ashton-Griffiths (*Lestrade*), Earl Rhodes (*Dudley Badcock*), Brian Oulton (*Master Snelgrove*), Patrick Newell (*Bentley Bobster*), Donald Eccles (*Reverend Duncan Nesbitt*), Matthew Ryan, Matthew Blakstead and Jonathan Lacey (*Dudley's Friends*), Walter Sparrow (*Ethan Engel*), Nadim Sawalha (*Egyptian Tavern Owner*), Roger Brierly (*Mr Holmes*), Vivienne Chandler (*Mrs Holmes*), Lockwood West (*Curio Shop Owner*), John Scott Martin (*Cemetery Caretaker*), George Malpas (*School Porter*), Willoughby Goddard (*School Reverend*), and the voice of Michael Hordern (*Older Watson*)
109 mins

1987

Tin Men

Baltimore, 1963. After quarrelling with his wife, Nora, an angry Ernest Tilley crashes into a brand-new Cadillac driven by Bill Babowsky. Furious at each other, they realize they are both aluminium-siding salesmen, though Bill is the more successful, thanks to his skills as a con-artist. Ernest proceeds to wreck

72 *Young Sherlock Holmes* (1985): Christopher Columbus, Steven Spielberg, and the Baltimore Pictures partners, Barry Levinson and Mark Johnson

Bill's loan car, while Bill seduces Nora and then tells Ernest over the telephone. A relieved Ernest throws Nora out, and she moves in with a reluctant Bill. Nora discovers her part in the feud and walks out on a now-changed Bill, who vents his despair in a drunken scuffle with Ernest. Bill convinces Nora he loves her, but Ernest refuses a divorce, instead challenging Bill to a game of pool to decide who should keep her. Bill loses. Meanwhile, both Bill and Ernest are made to face the Home Improvements Commission, who have inside information on their dubious business practices. Both lose their licences, but are reconciled when Ernest begs Bill to take care of Nora.

Production company: Touchstone in association with Silver Screen Partners II
Producer: Mark Johnson
Director: Barry Levinson
Screenplay: Barry Levinson
Photography: Peter Sova
Editor: Stu Linder
Production designer: Peter Jamison
Music: David Steele, Andy Cox, Fine Young Cannibals
Cast: Richard Dreyfuss (*Bill 'B. B.' Babowsky*), Danny DeVito (*Ernest Tilley*), Barbara Hershey (*Nora Tilley*), John Mahoney (*Moe*), Jackie Gayle (*Sam*), Stanley Brock (*Gil*), Seymour Cassel (*Cheese*), Bruno Kirby (*Mouse*), J. T. Walsh (*Wing*), Richard Portnow (*Carly*), Matt Craven (*Looney*), Alan Blumenfeld (*Stanley*), Brad Sullivan (*Masters*), Michael Tucker (*Bagel*), Deirdre O'Connell (*Nellie*), Sheila McCauley (*Ada*), Michael S. Willis (*Mr Shrubner*), Penny Nichols (*Mrs Shrubner*), Susan Duvall (*Suburban Housewife*), David DeBoy (*Suburban Husband*), Florence Moody (*Diner Waitress*), Myron Citrenbaum (*Murray*), Ralph Tabakin (*Mr Hudson*), Norma Posner (*Mrs Hudson*), Walt McPherson (*Cadillac Salesman*)
112 mins

1987

Good Morning, Vietnam

Saigon, 1965. Airman Adrian Cronauer arrives to host a morning show on the local Armed Forces Radio network. He immediately replaces the old style of MOR music and army bulletins with rock 'n' roll favourites, broken up with manic comic routines parodying the news service. His colleagues are delighted, but the humourless Lieutenant Hawk and authoritarian Sergeant-Major Dickerson oppose him. Cronauer is attracted to a Vietnamese girl, Trinh, and takes over English classes to meet her. Trinh's brother Tuan tries to discourage him, but Cronauer befriends Tuan and a day out for the couple is arranged, with her family in tow. When a bomb goes off at Jimmy Wah's bar, a local GI hangout, Cronauer defies censorship and broadcasts the news, so that even the sympathetic General Taylor is obliged to replace him with aspiring DJ Lieutenant Hawk. Hawk is a disaster, but even though Cronauer is reinstated he goes into a depression when he is told by Trinh a relationship is impossible. Dickerson sends Cronauer and his assistant Garlick into the field to interview GIs, and they narrowly escape the Vietcong with the unexpected help of Tuan. Dickerson informs Cronauer that his saviour is a known Vietcong saboteur responsible for the bomb at Jimmy Wah's, and that the DJ is being shipped out. General Taylor has his revenge by posting Dickerson to Guam. Before Cronauer leaves, he conducts an impromptu softball game with his devoted class of Vietnamese.

Production company: Touchstone in association with Silver Screen Partners III
Producers: Mark Johnson, Larry Brezner
Director: Barry Levinson
Screenplay: Mitch Markowitz
Photography: Peter Sova
Editor: Stu Linder
Production designer: Roy Walker
Music: Alex North
Cast: Robin Williams (*Airman Adrian Cronauer*), Forest Whitaker (*Private Edward Garlick*), Tung Thanh Tran (*Tuan*), Chintara Sukapatana (*Trinh*), Bruno Kirby (*Lieutenant Steven Hawk*), Robert Wuhl (*Marty Lee Dreiwitz*), J. T. Walsh (*Sergeant-Major Dickerson*), Noble Willingham (*General Taylor*), Richard Edson (*Private Abersold*), Juney Smith (*Phil McPherson*), Richard Portnow (*Dan 'The Man' Levitan*), Floyd Vivino (*Eddie Kirk*), Cu Ba Nguyen (*Jimmy Wah*), Mark Johnson (*Sergeant Sloan*), Dan R. Stanton (*1st Censor*), Don E. Stanton (*2nd Censor*), Danny Aiello III (*1st MP*), J. J. (*2nd MP*), James McIntire (*1st Sergeant at Jimmy Wah's*), Peter MacKenzie (*2nd Sergeant at Jimmy Wah's*)
108 mins

1988

Rain Man

As salesman Charlie Babbitt's business spirals into trouble with impounded cars and a bridging loan due, he receives the news that his father has died in Cincinnati. Explaining to his girlfriend Susanna that he left home when a teenager, he is nevertheless shocked to be bequeathed only a 1949 Buick Roadmaster convertible. The estate of $3 million goes to an unnamed beneficiary, whom Charlie tracks down to the Wallbrook Home for the Mentally Handicapped, only to discover that he has an autistic brother, Raymond, who was institutionalized when Charlie was two. Despite the great difficulties in communication, Charlie persuades Raymond to leave with him and Susanna for Los Angeles. But Susanna is appalled that Charlie is only after his share of the inheritance, and she walks out on him. Finding that the home's director, Dr Bruner, has no legal custody of Raymond, and unable to demand a ransom, Charlie takes Raymond away with him. However, their journey is complicated by Raymond's refusal to fly, take major highways, or travel when it is raining. Gradually some kind of rapport is established, and Charlie realizes that Raymond was the imaginary friend of his childhood, the 'rain man'. When Charlie's customers pull out their money because of non-delivery of their new cars, Charlie uses Raymond's abilities to win a fortune in Las Vegas, where they are reunited with Susanna. In Los Angeles, Charlie rejects the home's offer of $250,000 to return Raymond, wishing to care for him personally. But at the custody hearing he realizes that Raymond will be lost in the outside world, and gives him up to Dr Bruner.

Production company: United Artists/Guber-Peters Company
Producers: Peter Guber, Jon Peters, Mark Johnson
Director: Barry Levinson
Screenplay: Ronald Bass, Barry Morrow
Photography: John Seale
Editor: Stu Linder
Production designer: Ida Random
Music: Hans Zimmer
Cast: Dustin Hoffman (*Raymond Babbitt*), Tom Cruise (*Charlie Babbitt*), Valeria Golino (*Susanna*), Jerry Molen (*Dr Bruner*), Jack Murdock (*John Mooney*), Michael D. Roberts (*Vern*), Ralph Seymour (*Lenny*), Lucinda Jenney (*Iris*), Bonnie Hunt (*Sally Dibbs*), Kim Robillard (*Small-town Doctor*), Beth Grant (*Mother at Farmhouse*), Dolan Dougherty, Marshall Dougherty, Patrick Dougherty, John-Michael Dougherty, Peter Dougherty and Andrew Dougherty (*Farmhouse Kids*), Loretta Wendt Jolivette (*Dr Bruner's Secretary*), Donald E. Jones (*Minister at Funeral*), Bryon P. Caunar (*Man in Waiting Room*), Donna J. Dickson (*Nurse*), Earl Roat (*Man at Wallbrook Road*), William J. Montgomery Jnr (*Wallbrook Patient Entering TV Room*), Elizabeth Lower (*Bank Officer*), Michael C. Hall, Robert W. Heckel and W. Todd Kenner (*Police Officers at Accident*), Kneeles Reeves (*Amarillo Hotel Owner*), Jack W. Cope (*Irate Driver*), Nick Mazzola (*Blackjack Dealer*), Ralph Tabakin (*Shift Boss*), Ray Baker (*Kelso*)
133 mins

1990

Avalon

At the Thanksgiving gathering of the Krichinsky family, Sam tells the children the family history: how he arrived in America in 1914, believing that the Fourth of July celebrations were for him; how he joined his four brothers in the paperhanging business in Baltimore; and how he met his wife, Eva. Sam's son Jules, a door-to-door salesman, is attacked one night while out with his little boy, Michael. To help him recover, the family buys him the latest wonder, a television set. Jules then opens a TV store with his cousin Izzy, and moves his family out of the Avalon district and into the suburbs. Sam and Eva reluctantly join them, and Izzy and family move to across the street. One hot summer night, Sam tells them how he once owned a night-club, where Jules turned up to announce his sudden marriage to Ann, and how he and Izzy had changed their names to Kaye and Kirk. The cousins expand into a general appliance store, promising the lowest prices, and are highly successful. But the family is split up when, at Thanksgiving, Gabriel, one of the brothers, turns up late yet again to discover that this time they have lost patience and already cut the turkey. Izzy persuades Jules to start a vast discount warehouse, but the Fourth of July opening is ruined when the building burns down that night. Michael and Izzy's son Teddy mistakenly believe they are responsible, but far worse is the revelation that Izzy has spent the money set aside for the insurance premium on advertising. Ann becomes pregnant, and Sam and Eva go to live with her younger brother, Simka. Eva dies, the family continues to break up, and an enfeebled Sam moves in again with Jules, who now sells TV advertising, and his new son, David. Years later Sam is visited in a home by a grown-up Michael and his son Sam, and he begins to recount again his stories of Avalon to the distracted young boy.

Production company: Baltimore Pictures for Tri-Star Pictures
Producers: Barry Levinson, Mark Johnson
Director: Barry Levinson
Screenplay: Barry Levinson
Photography: Allen Daviau
Production designer: Norman Reynolds
Editor: Stu Linder
Music: Randy Newman
Cast: Armin Mueller-Stahl (*Sam Krichinsky*), Elizabeth Perkins (*Ann Kaye*), Joan Plowright (*Eva Krichinsky*), Kevin Pollak (*Izzy Kirk*), Aidan Quinn (*Jules Kaye*), Leo Fuchs (*Hymie Krichinsky*), Eve Gordon (*Dottie Kirk*), Lou Jacobi (*Gabriel Krichinsky*), Israel Rubinek (*Nathan Krichinsky*), Elijah Wood (*Michael Kaye*), Grant Gelt (*Teddy Kirk*), Mindy Loren Isenstein (*Mindy Kirk*), Shifra Lerer (*Nellie Krichinsky*), Mina Bern (*Alice Krichinsky*), Frania Rubinek (*Faye Krichinsky*), Neil Kirk (*Herbie*), Ronald Guttman (*Simka*), Rachel Aviva (*Elka*), Sylvia Weinberg (*Mrs Parkes*), Ralph Tabakin (*Principal Dunn*), Steve Aronson (*Moving Man*), Miles A. Perman (*Gas Attendant*), Beatrice Yoffe (*Nursing Home Receptionist*), Brian Sher (*Country Club Page*), Frank Tamburo (*Mugger*), Patrick Flynn (*Fire Chief*), Herb Levinson (*Rabbi at Funeral*)
128 mins

1991

Bugsy
Together with Meyer Lansky and Charlie 'Lucky' Luciano, Benjamin 'Bugsy' Siegel runs the rackets in New York. Leaving his wife, Esta, and their two daughters behind, Bugsy is sent by his partners to Los Angeles. An arch womanizer, Bugsy also demonstrates his cold-bloodedness by shooting a defaulting bookmaker, as well as his loyalty by lending money to Harry Greenberg, who is under pressure to name names to the law. In Los Angeles he is welcomed by his old friend, the actor George Raft, and on the set of one of his films Bugsy is immediately attracted to a beautiful but tough extra, Virginia Hill. Establishing himself among the glamorous set, Bugsy fantasizes about assassinating Mussolini, whom he believes he can meet through an admirer, the Countess di Frasso. He successfully persuades local racketeer Jack Dragna to

join his mob, and then recruits the bullish Mickey Cohen to run his West Coast operation. Finding out he is being swindled by Dragna, Bugsy humiliates him in a violent rage. Virginia now falls completely in love with Bugsy, despite his reluctance to obtain a divorce from Esta. On a trip to check out a run-down joint in Nevada, Bugsy has the idea of building up Las Vegas into a gambling empire. Virginia loses patience with Bugsy and finds other lovers. Back in New York for his elder daughter's birthday party, Bugsy is visited by Lansky and friends and he sells them the idea of Las Vegas. While Bugsy's marriage is falling apart, he persuades Virginia to join him in his venture, which, once started, becomes more and more costly. Harry Greenberg turns up, confesses he has squealed on his friends, and accepts that Bugsy must kill him. The costs of the Flamingo casino continue to rise, and Charlie Luciano pulls out. With only Lansky supporting him, Bugsy is arrested for the Greenberg killing, and word gets out that Virginia has diverted some of the money to a Swiss bank account. Freed from jail with help from a corrupt DA, Bugsy prepares a gala Christmas Day opening for the Flamingo, but it is a disaster. Lansky is no longer able to defend Bugsy to his colleagues, and though Virginia hands over the diverted money to Bugsy, he returns to Los Angeles and is shot dead.

Production company: Mulholland Productions/Baltimore Pictures for Tri-Star Pictures
Producers: Mark Johnson, Barry Levinson, Warren Beatty
Director: Barry Levinson
Screenplay: James Toback
Photography: Allen Daviau
Editor: Stu Linder
Production designer: Dennis Gassner
Music: Ennio Morricone
Cast: Warren Beatty (*Benjamin 'Bugsy' Siegel*), Annette Bening (*Virginia Hill*), Harvey Keitel (*Mickey Cohen*), Ben Kingsley (*Meyer Lansky*), Elliot Gould (*Harry Greenberg*), Joe Mantegna (*George Raft*), Richard Sarafian (*Jack Dragna*), Bebe Neuwirth (*Countess di Frasso*), Gian-Carlo Scandiuzzi (*Count di Frasso*), Wendy Phillips (*Esta Siegel*), Stefanie Mason (*Millicent Siegel*), Kimberly McCullough (*Barbara Siegel*), Andy Romano (*Del Webb*), Robert Beltran (*Alejandro*), Bill Graham (*Charlie 'Lucky' Luciano*), Lewis Van Bergen (*Joey Adonis*), Joseph Roman (*Moe Sedway*), James Toback (*Gus Greenbaum*), Don Carrara (*Vito Genovese*), Carmine Carida (*Frank Costello*), Don Calfa (*Louis Dragna*), Robert Glaudini (*Dominic*), Bryan Smith (*Chick Hill*), Ray McKinnon (*David Hinton*), Eric Christmas (*Ronald the Butler*), Joe Baker (*Lawrence Tibbett*), John C. Moskoff (*Sulka's Salesman*), Ralph Tabakin (*Elevator Operator*), Debrah Farentino (*Girl in Elevator*), Anthony Russell (*Jerry the Bookie*)
135 mins

1992

Toys

Before he dies, Kenneth Presswell, president of Panda Toys, Inc., hands over the family toy business to his brother, General Leland Presswell, rather than his devoted son and daughter, Leslie and Alsatia. Secretly he wants his children to face the challenge of their uncle's militaristic attitude. The General, however, has more than a few changes in mind, for he sees a way of manufacturing toys that will be as effective as real military weapons, but a lot cheaper.

Production company: Baltimore Pictures for 20th Century Fox
Producers: Mark Johnson, Barry Levinson
Director: Barry Levinson
Screenplay: Valerie Curtin, Barry Levinson
Photography: Adam Greenberg
Editor: Stu Linder
Production designer: Ferdinando Scarfiotti
Music: Hans Zimmer, Trevor Horn
Cast: Robin Williams (*Leslie Presswell*), Michael Gambon (*General Leland Presswell*), Joan Cusack (*Alsatia Presswell*), Robin Wright (*Gwen Tyler*), Donald O'Connor (*Kenneth Presswell*), Owens (*Arthur Malet*), L. L. Cool J (*Patrick Presswell*), Jack Warden (*General Presswell Snr*), Debi Mazir (*Debbie*)

A Note on the Editor

David Thompson worked in film distribution and exhibition before becoming a freelance journalist and joining the BBC in 1983. There he has programmed film seasons and produced the series 'The Film Club'. More recently he has directed documentaries on Roberto Rossellini and Peter Greenaway, as well as contributing reports to the BBC series 'Moving Pictures'. He was co-editor of *Scorsese on Scorsese*.

Index